BEGINNING KEYBOARDING

The Sidewalk Labs Method

Designed for Jr/Sr High School Classroom Instruction

STUDENT NAME:

____

STUDENT WORKBOOK

2024 EDITION

A Sidewalk Labs Education Book
Student Workbook v1

All inquiries should be addressed in email to publisher@sidewalklabs.net.
www.sidewalklabs.net

ISBN: 978-1-955732-01-7

Section I: KEYBOARDING RESOURCES

Glossary

Word	Definition	Index

Word	Definition	Index

Repertoire List

TITLE	FOCUS	LEVEL

TITLE	FOCUS	LEVEL

Reading the Staff

Study Guide

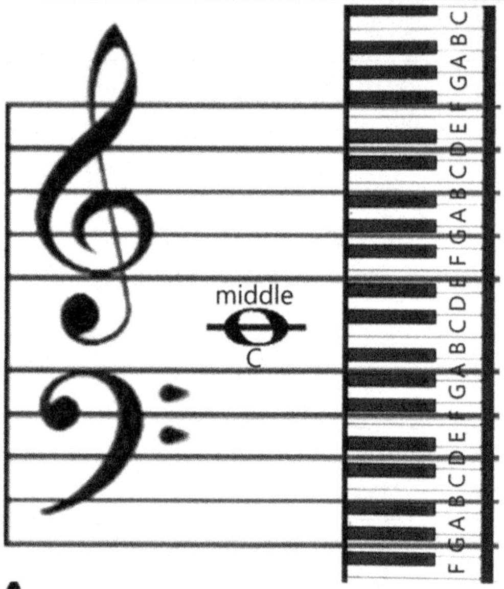

The piano staff aligns directly with the keys of the keyboard.

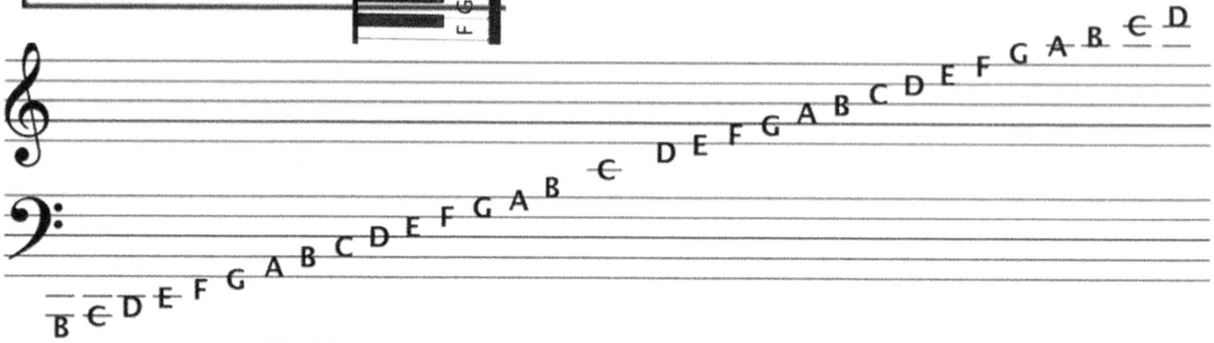

Because piano players have to find the notes very quickly, it helps to learn **mnemonic devices** (memory tricks) to remember them, such as words or phrases to quickly identify lines or spaces.

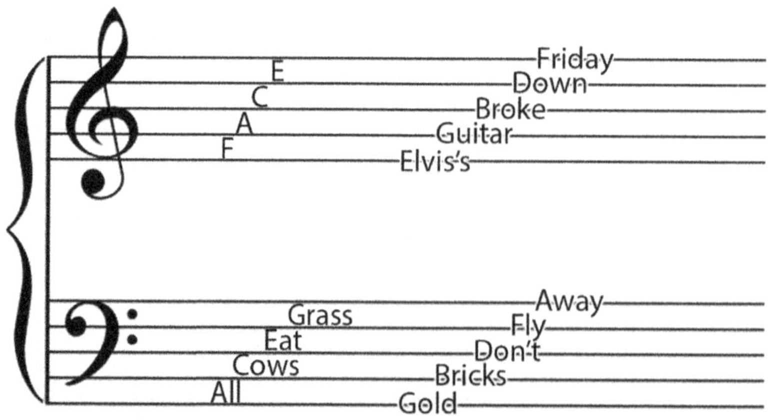

(doodle space)

Sample Note-Reading Test

The following note arrangements spell words. Write the letters under the notes to decode the words on the staff. Remember to check the clef.

Sample Level 1 Analysis Test

Questions: (music on next page)
What is the **title** of the piece?
Who **composed** it?
How many **measures**?
For **measures 1 and 2**, write the letters next to the **notes** in both right and left hand.
How many **beats** in each **measure**?
How should you play **measures 13 and 14**? (choose the correct answer) 1. extra slowly 2. start quiet and gradually get louder 3. legato, or smooth and connected 4. staccato, or very short and separated
The note that has both an **accent mark** and a **staccato mark** is which letter?
Most of the **notes** and **rests** are which kind? 1. whole notes and rests 2. half notes and rests 3. quarter notes and rests 4. eighth notes and rests
The **note** in the right hand that has a **fermata mark** is which letter?
Is the curved line in the right hand of measures 15 and 16 a **slur** or a **tie**? 1. slur 2. tie

Hickory Dickory Dock

Sample Level 1 Analysis Test

Questions: (music on next page)
What is the **title** of the piece?
How many years ago was the **composer** born?
How many **measures**?
For **measures 10 and 11**, write the letters next to the **notes** in both right and left hand.
What is the **articulation** in the **first three measures**?
What is the **loudest measure(s)**?
How many **ties** appear in the piece?
The most common **rhythm** in the left hand is which **type of note**?
Draw a box around a **treble clef**.
What is the **highest note** in the piece?

Waltz in C Major

Op. 82, No. 18

Cornelius Gurlitt
(1820-1901)

17
mp
21
25
29

Sample Level 2 Analysis Test

Questions:
What **period** of music does this piece represent?
Who **arranged** the piece for piano study?
How many **beats per measure**?
In measure 2 write the letters next to the **notes** in both right and left hand.
What is the **articulation** in the right hand in measure 7?
What **key** is it in?
Is the curved line in measure 6 a **slur** or a **tie**?
Draw a box around the **repeat sign(s)**.
What is the **tempo** and what does it mean?
Circle an **accent mark**.

Ecossaise
WoO 23
Ludwig van Beethoven
(1770-1827)
arr. Carl Czerny
Allegro
p
5
9
f
13

Sample History Test

The four periods of music since 1600 are **Classical**, **Modern**, **Baroque**, **Romantic** Write them next to the appropriate years: 1600-1750 ______________________ 1750-1820 ______________________ 1820-1910 ______________________ 1910-2021 ______________________
Which of the periods experienced the largest growth in population?
Which of the periods used music to represent powerful emotions?
Wolfgang Amadeus Mozart was a significant composer from which period?
Johann Sebastian Bach was a significant composer from which period?
Which period had the largest orchestra?
Which period was known for enjoying innovation, experimentation, and technology?
In which period did the piano commonly appear in people's homes?
Art music in the 20th century included: 1. The development of the orchestra for the entertainment of the upper class 2. Music by educated, trained musicians applying modernism to western music 3. Rock, pop, R&B, soul and hip-hop 4. Most of the popular music that appeared on Billboard charts

Prepared piano is a form of:

1. Orchestra music
2. Parlor music from the Romantic Period
3. Exercise used for piano instruction
4. Experimental music from the Modern Period

From the following list, select any that are schools of modern **art music**.

1. Appalachian music
2. minimalism
3. serialism
4. disco
5. nationalism
6. romanticism
7. experimental music

Which of the following *most* contributed to the change from *folk music* to *popular music* and the appearance of what we would call **genres**?

1. The appearance of record labels and the Billboard charts
2. The march of Napoleon through Europe
3. The creation of electric and electronic instruments
4. The immigration of other cultures into the melting pot of the United States

From the following list, select any that are **genres** of modern **popular music.**

1. fugue
2. rock and roll
3. jazz
4. disco
5. country
6. opera
7. microtonism

(doodle space)

Mini-Concert Planning Sheet: Primer Songs

A **mini-concert** is a performance that helps performers grow and improve rather than focusing solely on entertaining the audience. It replicates a real performance as closely as possible, allowing students to practice and develop the physical, mental, and psychological skills needed for real-world performances. It serves as a stepping-stone to prepare students for the challenges of performing in front of others.

Use this sheet to plan and prepare for your first graded mini-concert.

You may perform additional pieces than required if you wish. You will be graded on your best work.

Requirements:	Due Date:
Both: • One primer level piece (minimum 8 measures) in the right hand. • One primer level piece (minimum 8 measures) in the left hand. **Or:** • One level 1 piece (minimum 8 measures) using both hands.	

Performance Selections:

Title	Hands/Level	Score
	Final Score:	

Mini-Concert Planning Sheet: 2 Level 1 Songs

A **mini-concert** is a performance that helps performers grow and improve rather than focusing solely on entertaining the audience. It replicates a real performance as closely as possible, allowing students to practice and develop the physical, mental, and psychological skills needed for real-world performances. It serves as a stepping-stone to prepare students for the challenges of performing in front of others.

Use this sheet to plan and prepare for your mini-concert.

You may perform additional pieces than required if you wish. You will be graded on your best work.

Requirements:	Due Date:

• **Two level 1 pieces.**
  ○ Lower level will be scored at -10 points per level.
  ○ Higher level will be scored at +5 points per level.
• If performing repertoire from outside the workbook, sheet music must be provided.	

Performance Selections:

Title	Level	Score
	Final Score:	

Scale Performance Scoring Sheet

For this performance, you will perform three scales. You may receive bonus points for using a metronome, for using both hands at the same time, or for extending past a single octave. Indicate how you intend to perform using the rubric below.

Scale Name:	
Tempo:	☐ 60-90bpm ☐ 90-120bpm ☐ 120+bpm ☐ with metronome
Hands:	☐ Right hand ☐ Left hand ☐ Both hands
Range:	☐ One octave ☐ Two octaves ☐ Three octaves or more
Scale Name:	
Tempo:	☐ 60-90bpm ☐ 90-120bpm ☐ 120+bpm ☐ with metronome
Hands:	☐ Right hand ☐ Left hand ☐ Both hands
Range:	☐ One octave ☐ Two octaves ☐ Three octaves or more
Scale Name:	
Tempo:	☐ 60-90bpm ☐ 90-120bpm ☐ 120+bpm ☐ with metronome
Hands:	☐ Right hand ☐ Left hand ☐ Both hands
Range:	☐ One octave ☐ Two octaves ☐ Three octaves or more

Mini-Concert Planning Sheet: 3 Level 1 Songs

A **mini-concert** is a performance that helps performers grow and improve rather than focusing solely on entertaining the audience. It replicates a real performance as closely as possible, allowing students to practice and develop the physical, mental, and psychological skills needed for real-world performances. It serves as a stepping-stone to prepare students for the challenges of performing in front of others.
Use this sheet to plan and prepare for your mini-concert.
You may perform additional pieces than required if you wish. You will be graded on your best work.

Requirements:	Due Date:

• **Three level 1 pieces**. (You may repeat pieces from a previous concert)
  ○ Lower level will be scored at -10 points per level.
  ○ Higher level will be scored at +5 points per level.
• If performing repertoire from outside the workbook, sheet music must be provided.	

Performance Selections:

Title	Level	Score
	Final Score:	

Mini-Concert Planning Sheet: Transposition

A **mini-concert** is a performance that helps performers grow and improve rather than focusing solely on entertaining the audience. It replicates a real performance as closely as possible, allowing students to practice and develop the physical, mental, and psychological skills needed for real-world performances. It serves as a stepping-stone to prepare students for the challenges of performing in front of others.

Use this sheet to plan and prepare for your mini-concert.

You may perform additional pieces than required if you wish. You will be graded on your best work.

Requirements:	Due Date:

• **One transposed level 1 piece.**
   o Lower level will be scored at --30 points per level.
   o Higher level will be scored at +10 points per level.
• If performing repertoire from outside the workbook, sheet music must be provided.	

Performance Selections:

Title	Keys	Score
	Final Score:	

Mini-Concert Planning Sheet: 5 Level 1 Songs

A **mini-concert** is a performance that helps performers grow and improve rather than focusing solely on entertaining the audience. It replicates a real performance as closely as possible, allowing students to practice and develop the physical, mental, and psychological skills needed for real-world performances. It serves as a stepping-stone to prepare students for the challenges of performing in front of others.

Use this sheet to plan and prepare for your mini-concert.

You may perform additional pieces than required if you wish. You will be graded on your best work.

Requirements:	Due Date:

• **Five level 1 pieces**. (You may repeat pieces from previous concerts)
  ○ Lower level will be scored at -20 points per level.
  ○ Higher level will be scored at +5 points per level.
• If performing repertoire from outside the workbook, sheet music must be provided.	

Performance Selections:

Title	Level	Score
	Final Score:	

Mini-Concert Planning Sheet: Variations

A **mini-concert** is a performance that helps performers grow and improve rather than focusing solely on entertaining the audience. It replicates a real performance as closely as possible, allowing students to practice and develop the physical, mental, and psychological skills needed for real-world performances. It serves as a stepping-stone to prepare students for the challenges of performing in front of others.

Use this sheet to plan and prepare for your mini-concert.

You may perform additional pieces than required if you wish. You will be graded on your best work.

Requirements:	Due Date:
• One piece (minimum level 1) with prepared variations. o Variations must be written in advance (see guidelines on worksheet). o Minimum of 8 measures.	

Performance Selections:

Title	Level	Score
	Final Score:	

Mini-Concert Planning Sheet: 7 Level 1 Songs

A **mini-concert** is a performance that helps performers grow and improve rather than focusing solely on entertaining the audience. It replicates a real performance as closely as possible, allowing students to practice and develop the physical, mental, and psychological skills needed for real-world performances. It serves as a stepping-stone to prepare students for the challenges of performing in front of others.

Use this sheet to plan and prepare for your mini-concert.

You may perform additional pieces than required if you wish. You will be graded on your best work.

Requirements:	Due Date:

• **Seven level 1 pieces**. (You may repeat pieces from previous concerts)
  o Lower level will be scored at -20 points per level.
  o Higher level will be scored at +5 points per level.
  o Transposed pieces will be scored at +5 points.
  o Pre-written variations will be scored at +10 points.
• If performing repertoire from outside the workbook, sheet music must be provided.	

Performance Selections:

Title	**Level**	**Score**
	Final Score:	

Mini-Concert Planning Sheet: Final Concert

A **mini-concert** is a performance that helps performers grow and improve rather than focusing solely on entertaining the audience. It replicates a real performance as closely as possible, allowing students to practice and develop the physical, mental, and psychological skills needed for real-world performances. It serves as a stepping-stone to prepare students for the challenges of performing in front of others.

Use this sheet to plan and prepare for your mini-concert.

You may perform additional pieces than required if you wish. You will be graded on your best work.

Requirements:	Due Date:
• **Ten pieces, minimum level 1, minimum 8 measures.** o Transposed pieces: +5 o Pre-listed variations: up to +10 o Higher level pieces: up to +10 o Longer pieces may count for multiple pieces (8 measures/piece)	

Performance Selections:

Title	Level	Score
	Final Score:	

Blank Staff Paper

Section II: KEYBOARDING LESSONS

Cycle of Mastery

Phases of Experience:
Multi-Iterative Circular Routines:

Internalization

Internalization:
Practice:
Study:

Post Questions:
Describe the meaning of **internalization** in your own words.
The process of internalizing something physical is referred to as:
The process of internalizing something mental is referred to as:
(doodle)

First Piece

The Music Alphabet:

The Piano Keyboard:

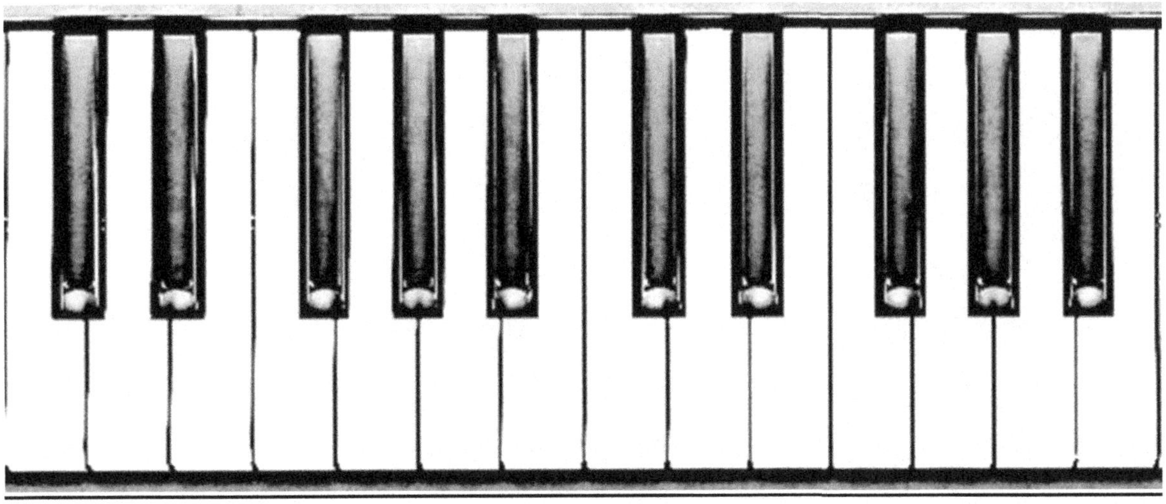

Finger Numbers:
(doodle space)

Layer 1: Notes

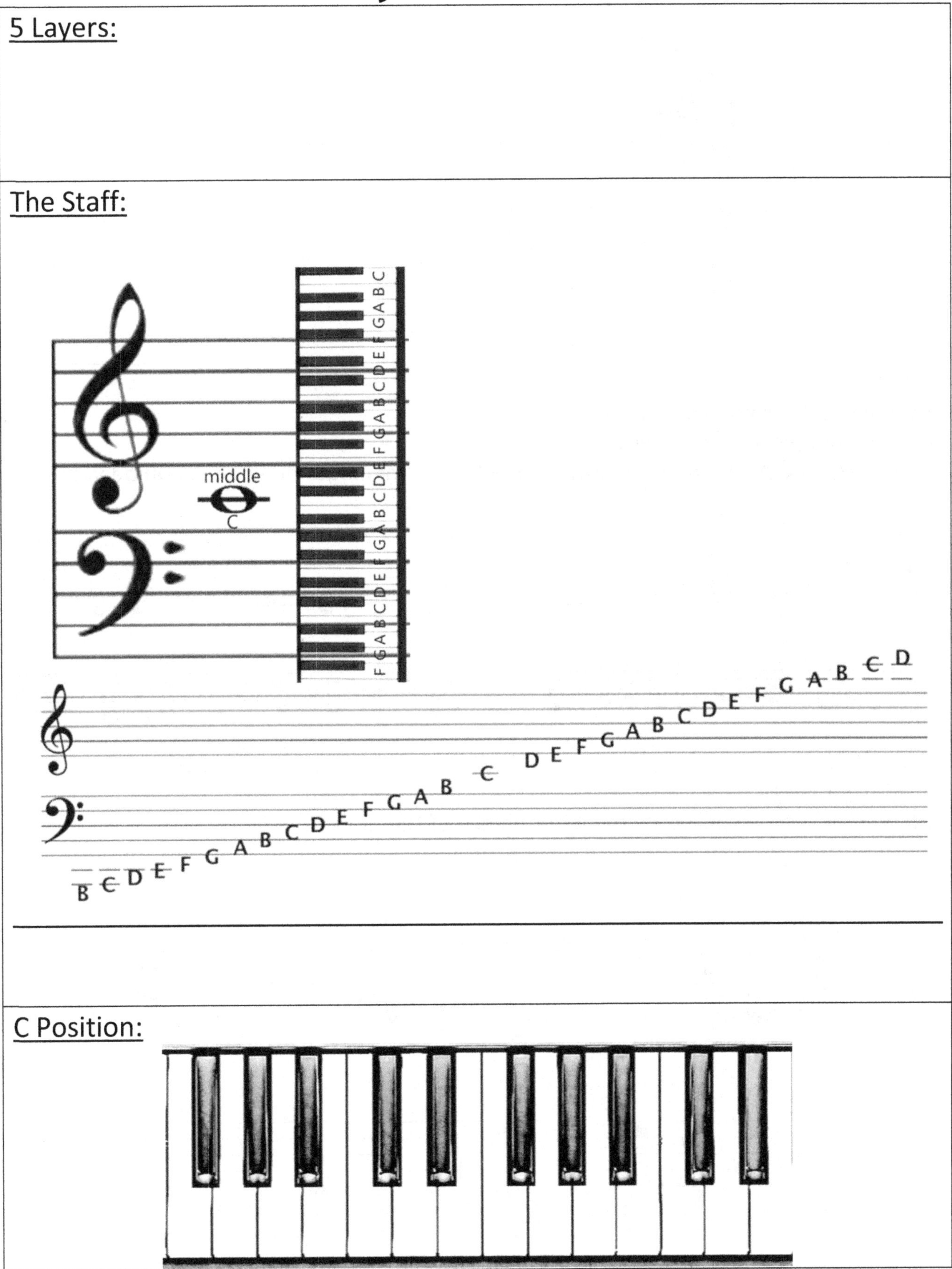

Staff Mnemonics:

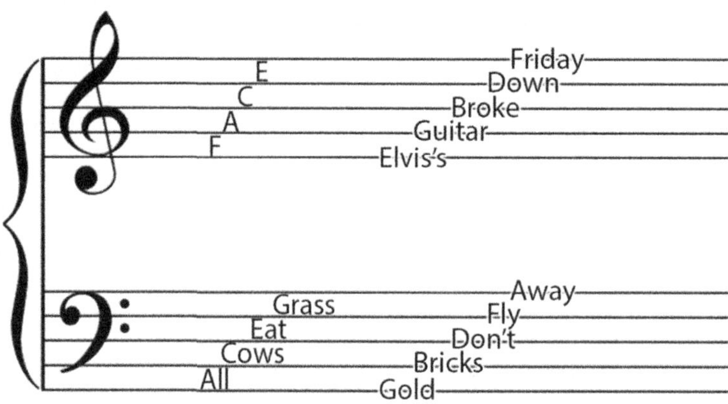

Practice:

Write the **letter names** below the notes.
Write the **finger numbers** below the notes.
Try to play in **C position** using either the letters or the finger numbers to guide you.

Reading Practice:

Decode the words spelled by the letter names of the notes.

Primer Level Songs

Are You Sleeping?
Jingle Bells
This Old Man
5 Little Indians

Active Practice

Idealized Routines:

Active Focuses:

Post Questions:
Are there any active practices you already regularly apply? If so, list them.
You should try one completely new active practice today. Which one did you choose?
How many times should you repeat the active practice before switching to a new one?
(doodle space)

Flats and Sharps

Black Keys:

Flats and Sharps:

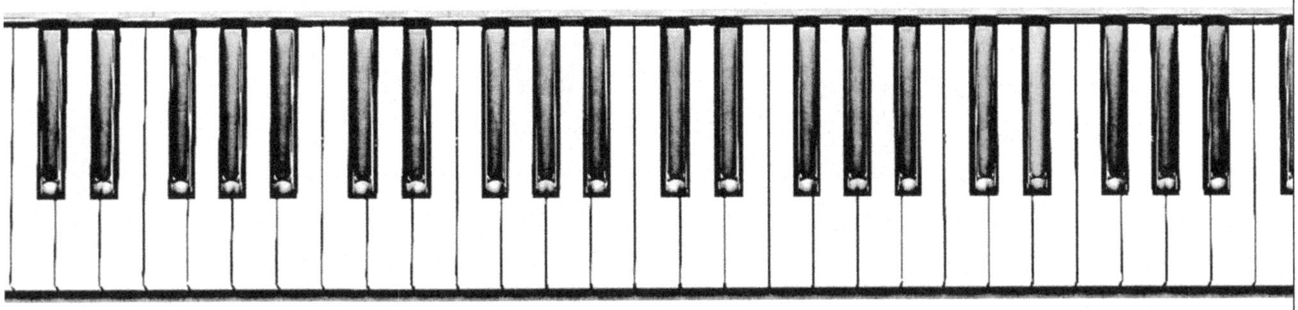

Reading Practice:

Decode the words spelled by the letter names of the notes.

Try writing in the names of these notes using sharps and flats.

(doodle space)

Leveling Up

Why Levels?

Skill Games:

Reading Practice:

Decode the words spelled by the letter names of the notes.

Ode to Joy

from *Symphony No. 9 in D minor*, Op. 125

Ludwig van Beethoven
(1770-1827)

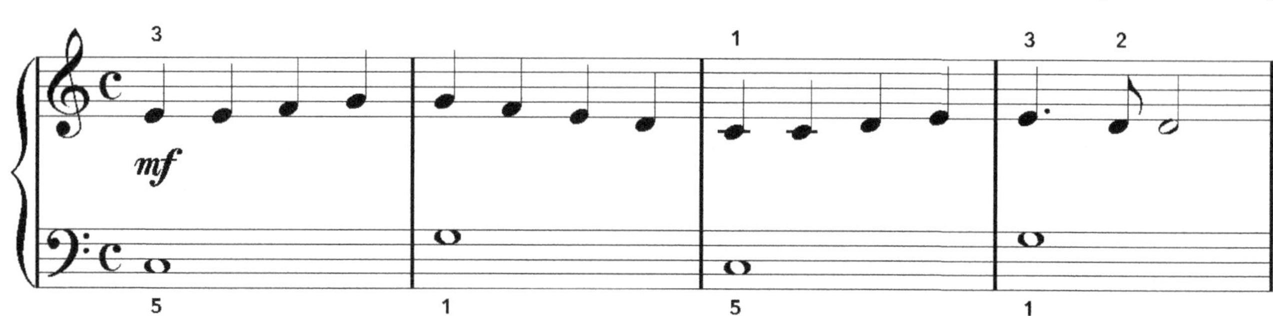

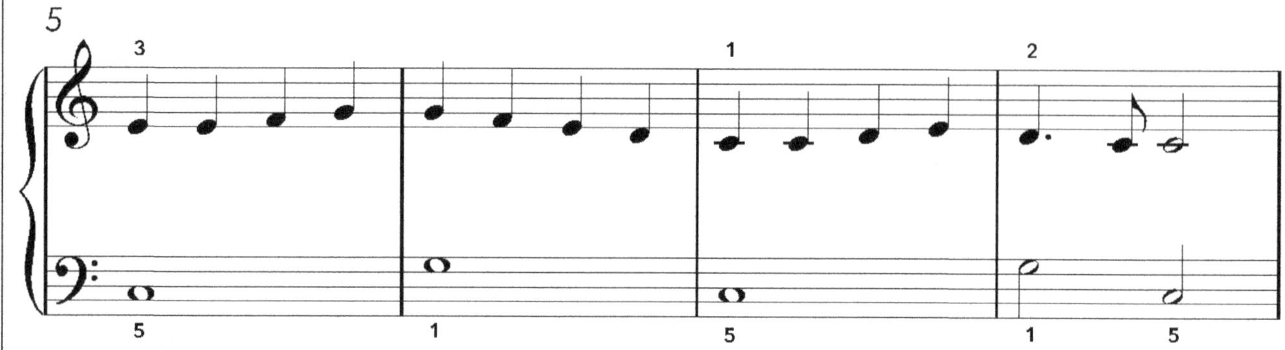

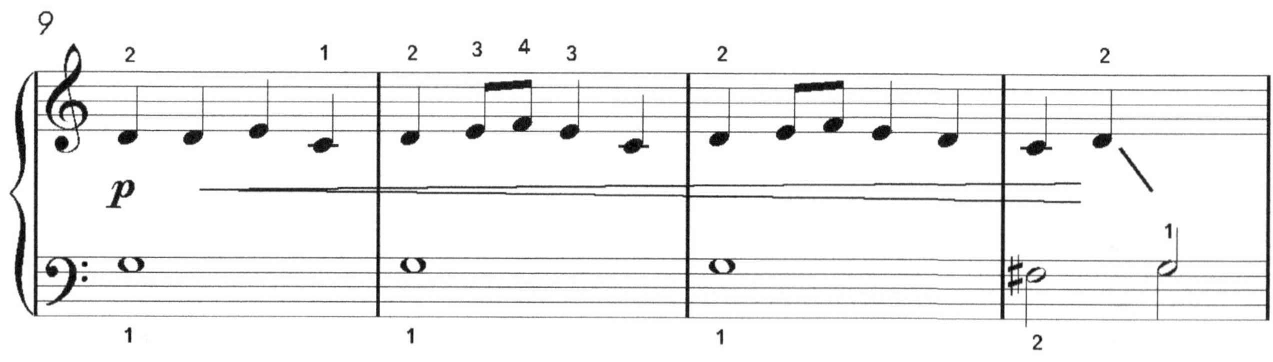

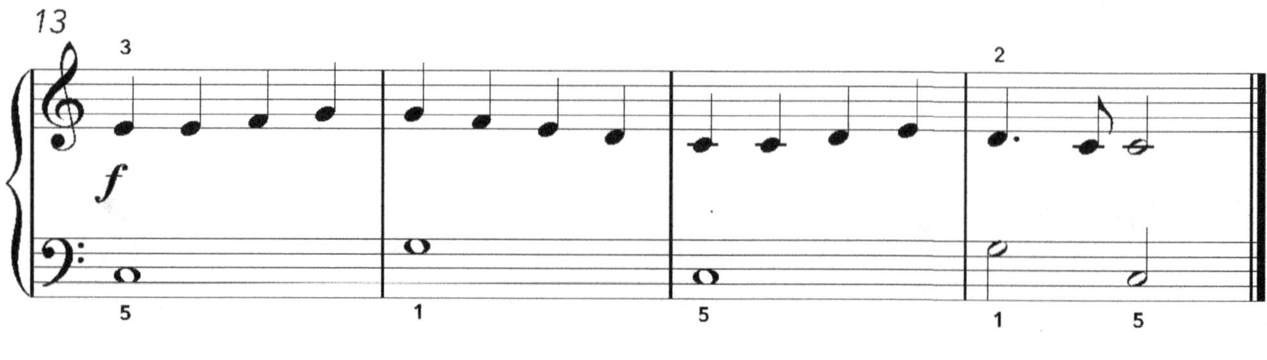

Layer 2: Rhythms

5 Layers Review:

Rhythm:

Rhythm Notation System:

Post Questions:

What is a **beat**?

How does adding each new "decoration" to the note change its length?

What is a **note head** with no other decorations called?

(doodle space)

Meter and Time Signatures

Rhythm Review:

Meter:

Time Signature:

Post Questions:
The word **meter** refers to a repeating pattern of what aspect of music?
Which part of a **time signature** tells you the **meter**?
What is the symbol for **common time**, the most frequently used **time signature**?

R	N	H	P	F	W	H	N	A	Z	L	V	H
H	T	N	E	E	T	X	I	S	X	Y	Z	X
G	W	Q	C	H	W	N	F	P	S	P	U	T
P	K	M	G	O	O	E	N	U	I	P	R	T
I	I	I	E	T	M	D	A	E	G	G	K	M
T	E	L	E	T	E	M	X	K	N	N	R	D
I	M	E	V	T	E	X	O	Y	A	I	L	T
M	W	V	T	N	G	R	P	N	T	M	H	A
E	H	O	S	T	R	O	N	G	U	I	A	E
C	D	W	H	O	L	E	U	A	R	T	L	B
M	H	T	Y	H	R	R	E	Y	E	V	F	S

weak dotted strong eighth timing meter
whole common rhythm signature sixteenth
time beat half note

Additional Rhythm Symbols

Rhythm Review:

The Dot:

The Tie:

Post Questions:

How does a **dot** affect the length of a note?

Draw two notes **tied** together on the staff below.

How long (for how many **beats**) should you hold the notes you drew on the above staff?

(doodle space)

Active Practice: Rhythm

Active Practice Review:

Active Practices for Internalizing Timing and Rhythm:

Choose some specific active practices to try this week:

____

____

____

____

____

Rhythm Math:

Try to solve the problems by replacing the symbols with the proper number of **beats**.
Assume the time signature is **common time**.

𝅝 + 𝅗𝅥 - ♩ = ________

♫ + 𝄽 + 𝅗𝅥. = ________

𝅗𝅥 - ♩ + 𝅗𝅥. = ________

𝅗𝅥 x 𝅝 = ________

(doodle space)

Middle C Position

Yankee Doodle

Traditional

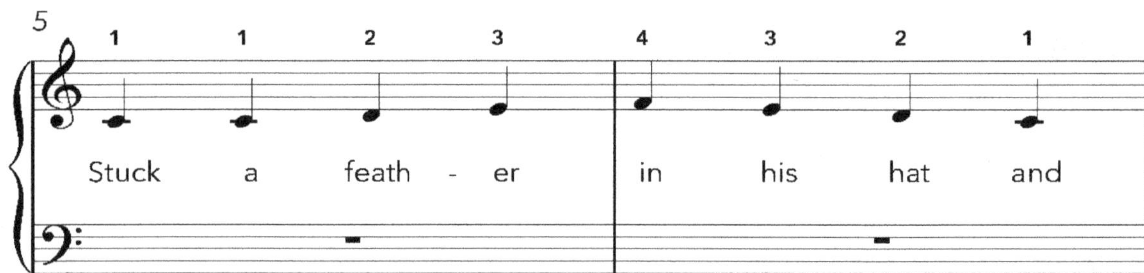

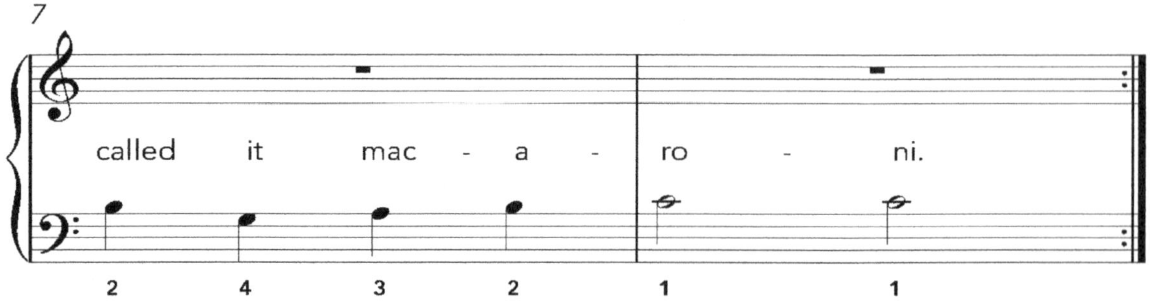

Post Questions:
What finger or fingers are placed on **middle C** in **middle C position**?
Going from left to right, which **notes** are covered by the fingers of each hands?

Layer 3: Dynamics

Five Layers Review:

Dynamics:

Italian Phrases:

Dynamics Symbols:

Rhythm Math:

Try to solve the problems by replacing the symbols with the proper number of **beats**.

Assume the time signature is **common time**.

♩ + ♩ = ___

♫ + ♩ = ___

𝅝 + ♫ = ___

𝅗𝅥 + 𝅝 = ___

D I M I N U E N D O H N U
F O D N E C S E R C E D M
O P I A N I S S I M O E O
R U I A E H P O P C Z L I
T P I A N O I L W Z V J A
E L S O F T E M O P E U T
E D O Y O D N E C S E R C
P O Y U A A T I A N G E C
U A P U D S C I M A N Y D
Q E I Q C P O R S I A T N
O M I S S I T R O F O N I

dynamics fortissimo crescendo mezzo

pianissimo decrescendo diminuendo

soft piano forte loud

Reading Methods

Staff to Keys:
Hand-by-Hand Reading:
Stack-by-Stack Reading:

Rhythm Math:

Try to solve the problems by replacing the symbols with the proper number of **beats**.

Assume the time signature is **common time**.

Sight-Reading Practice:

The following piece is in **middle C position**. Try using both methods to see if you can read it without having to write any of the notes into the music.

March in Middle C

C Major Position

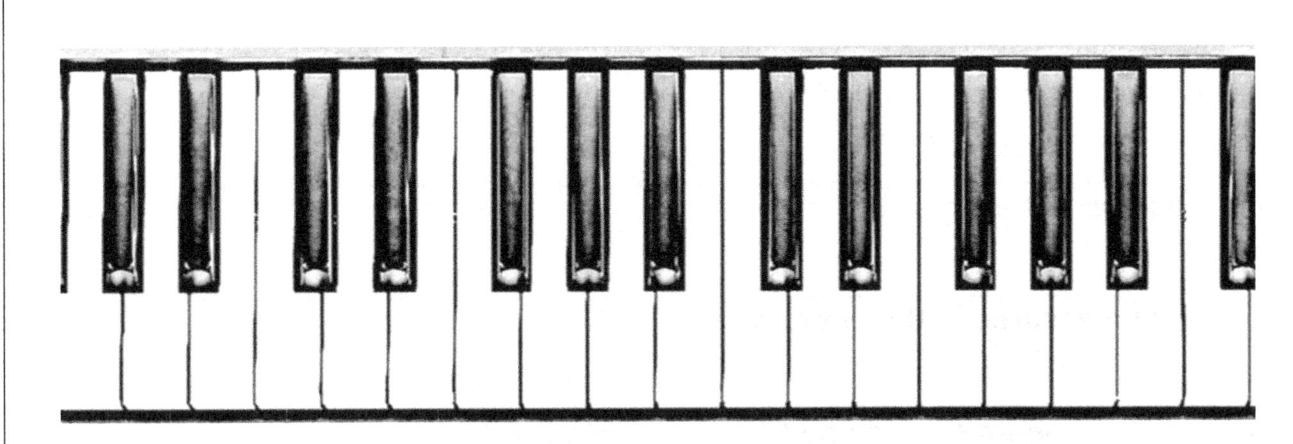

Bird By a River

Sidewalk Labs

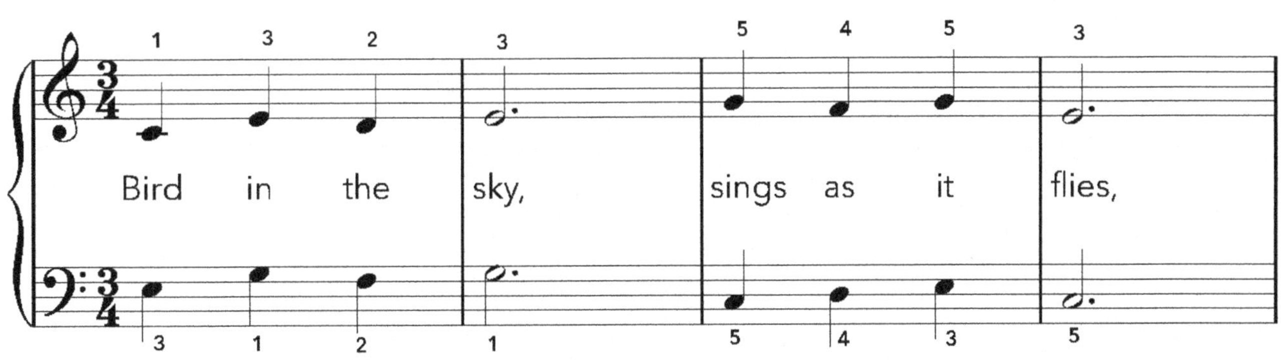

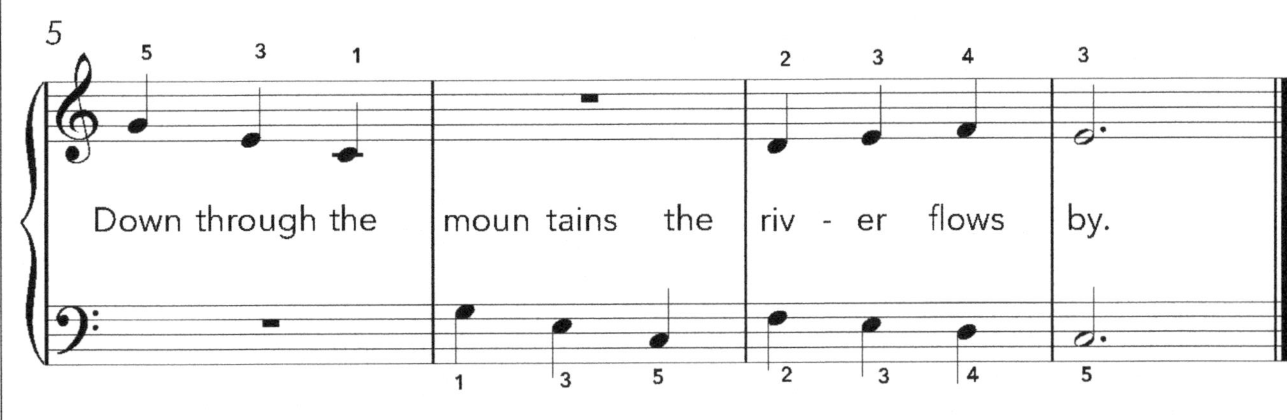

Analysis Questions:
What is the **first note** in the **right hand**?
What is the **first note** in the **left hand**?
What **position** is the song in?
How many **measures** in the entire song?
For how many **beats** should you hold the **final note**?
(doodle space)

Layer 4: Articulations

5 Layers Review:

Articulations:

Legato:

Staccato:

Non-Legato:

Accented:

Sight-Reading Practice:

The following piece is in **middle C position**. Try first **sight-reading** this simple piece using the information given. Then add **slurs**, **staccatos**, and **accents** as desired directly to the music. Try practicing it with your own added **articulations**.

Seven Gypsies

Sidewalk Labs

(doodle space)

G Major Position

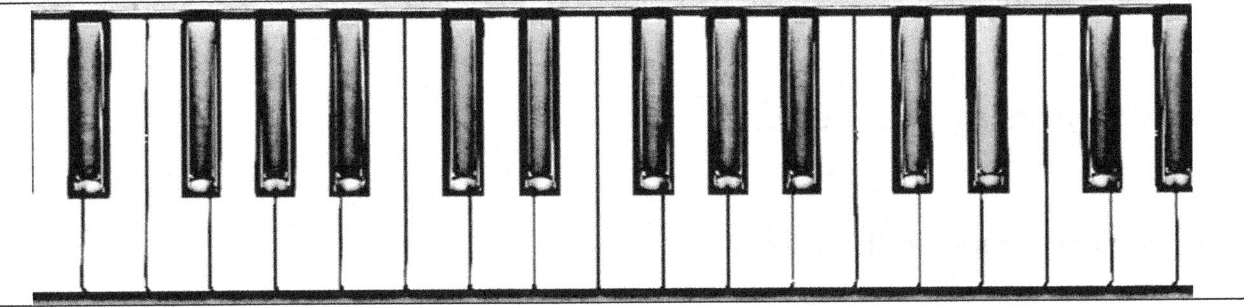

Faster! Faster! Like Children All Around

from *60 Progressive Pieces for Piano*,
Op. 60, No. 2

Daniel Gottlob Turk
(1756-1813)

Very fast

Analysis Questions:
Who is the **composer**?
How many years ago was he born?
How many **measures** in the piece?
How many **beats** in each measure?
There are only three different **notes** in the left hand. What are they?
(doodle space)

Mixed Positions

Mixed Positions:
Analysis Questions:
Who is the **composer**?
How many **measures**?
What kind of **rest** appears in the **final measure**?
What is the **position** of the **right hand**?
What is the **position** of the **left hand**?

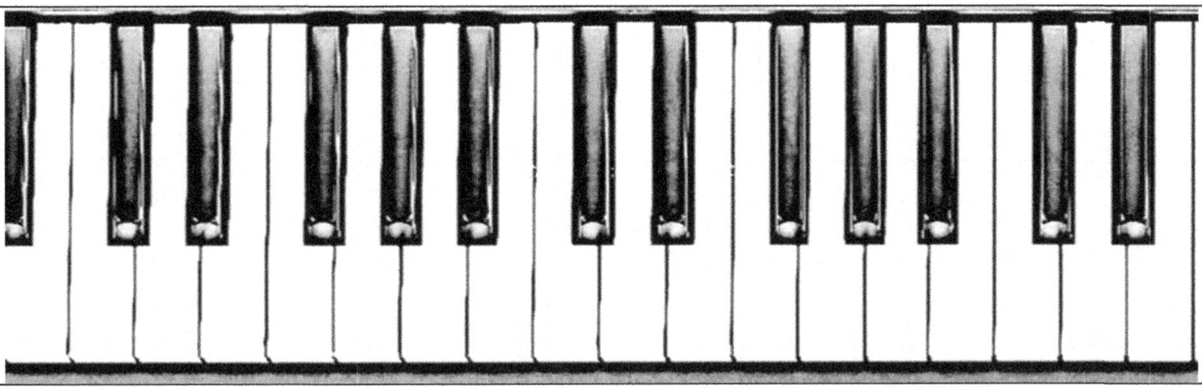

Twinkle, Twinkle Little Star

from the French folk tune "Ah! vous dirai-je, maman"
lyrics from the poem "The Star" by Jane Taylor

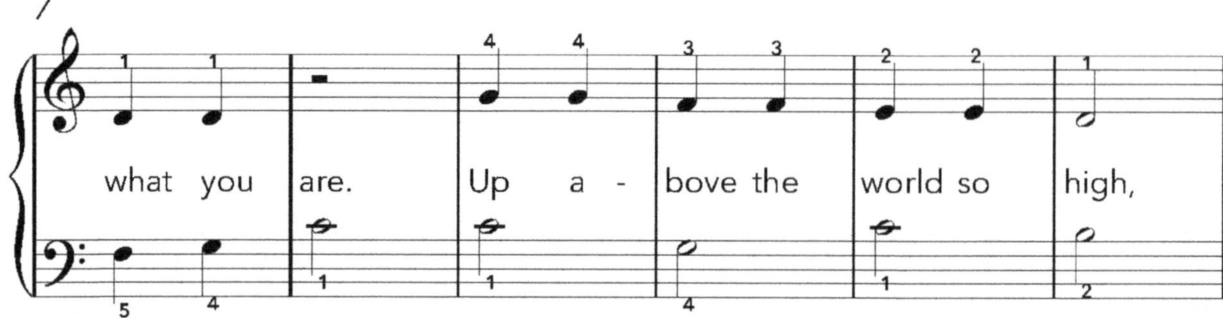

Key Signatures

Key Signatures:

Analysis Questions:

Who **composed** the piece?

What is the **position**?

Is the **articulation** throughout **legato**, **non-legato**, or **staccato**?

Circle the **time signature**. Put a box around the **key signature**.

Which **note(s)** should be adjusted because of the **key signature**?

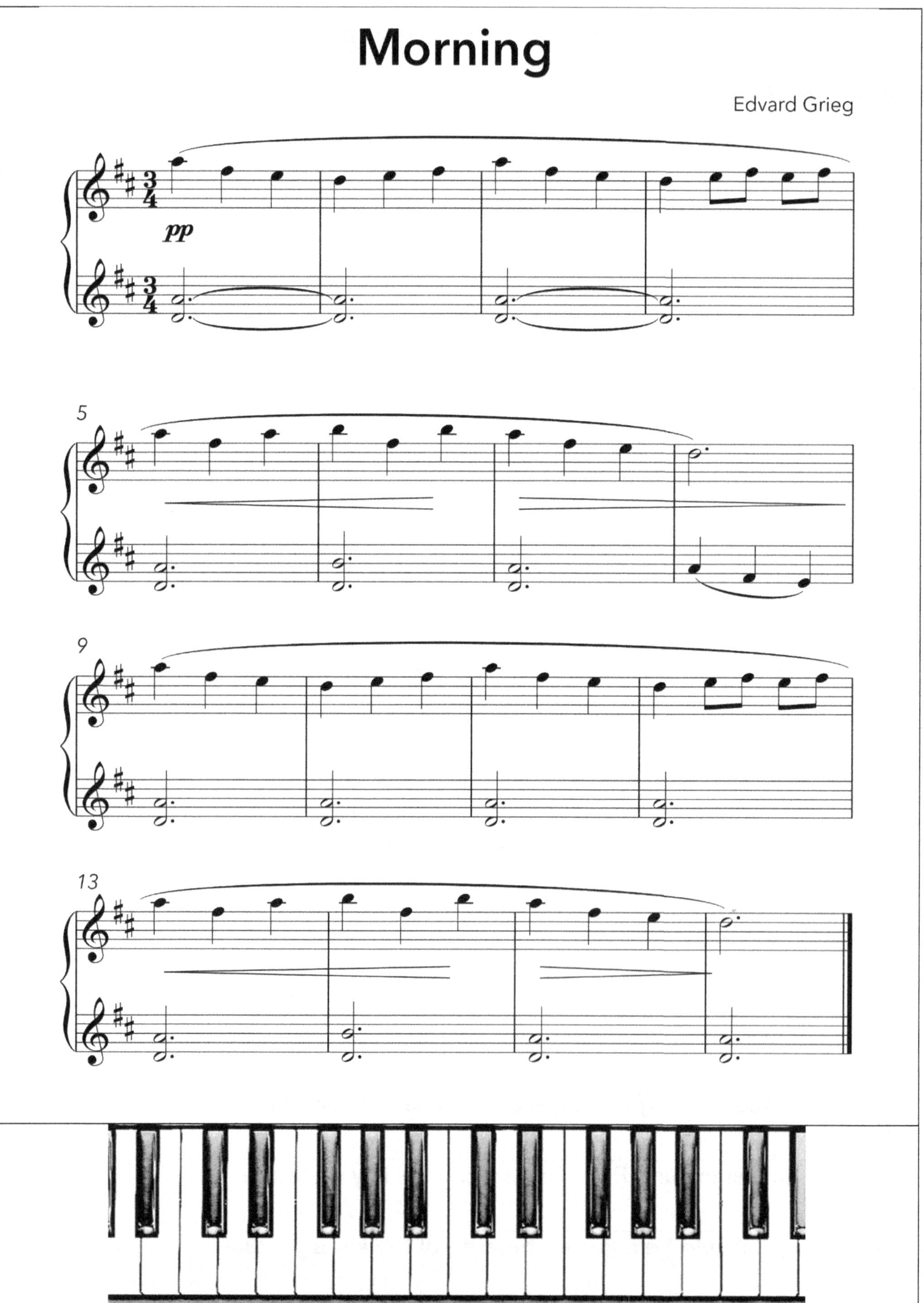
Morning
Edvard Grieg
pp
5
9
13

Rule of Flats and Sharps

Rule of Flats and Sharps:

Cautionary Symbols:

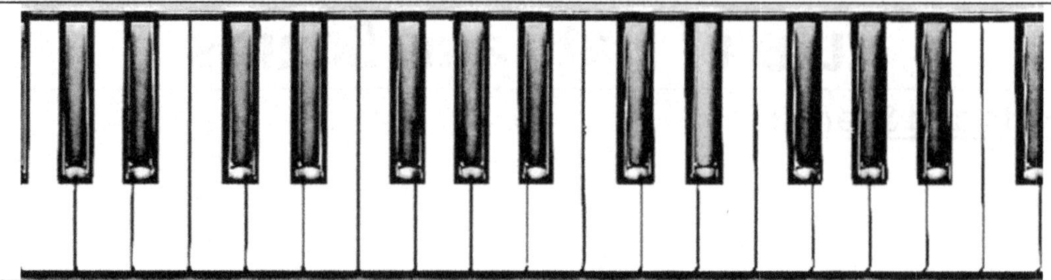

Bicycle Wheels

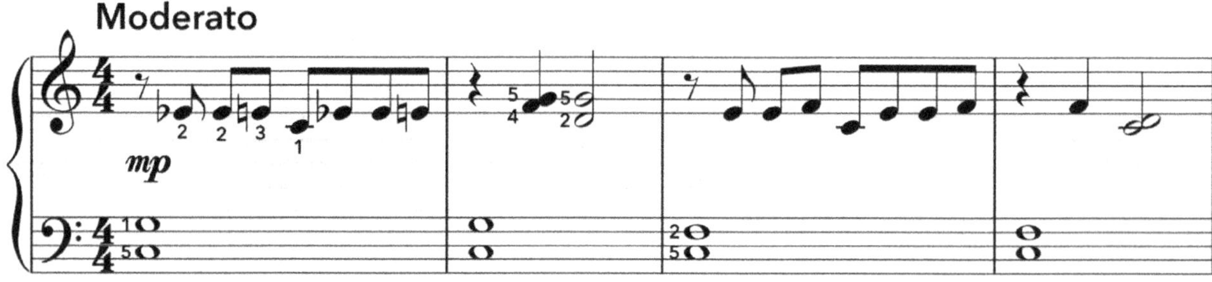

Analysis Questions:

What is the **tempo**?

Circle the **measure number(s)**.

Can you identify the **position**?

Keeping in mind the **rule of flats and sharps**, write in the notes in measure 8.

At what **dynamic** should the piece be played?

Layer 5: Flow and Expression

5 Layers Review:
Italian Tempos:
Fermata:
Analysis Questions:
What is the **position**?
How fast should the piece be played?
What is the **highest note** in the piece?
What **note(s)** should be adjusted due to the **key signature**?
Select one or two **notes** that you feel deserve a dramatic pause. Add a **fermata** to the music and practice it dramatically.

The Streets of Laredo

Traditional Folk Song

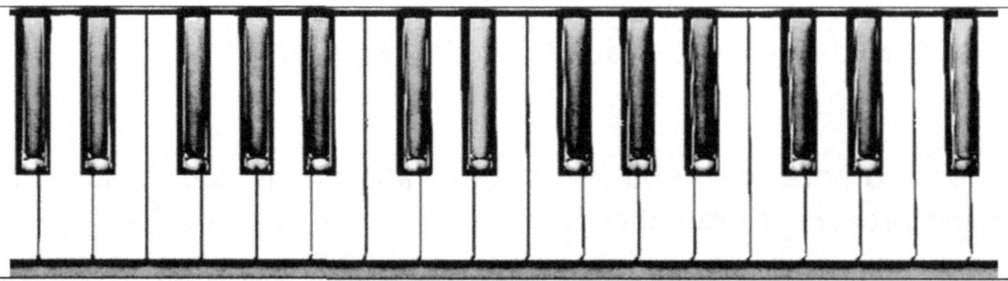

Repeats

Repeat Signs:

Other Repeats:

Analysis Questions:

How many **measures**?

What is the **tempo**?

Circle the **repeat sign(s)**.

How many **beats** in each **measure**?

What is the **articulation** throughout the piece?

Melody in C Major

Beyer: Lessons in Keyboard, Op. 101 No. 16

Ferdinand Beyer
(1803-1863)

Moderato

5

9

13

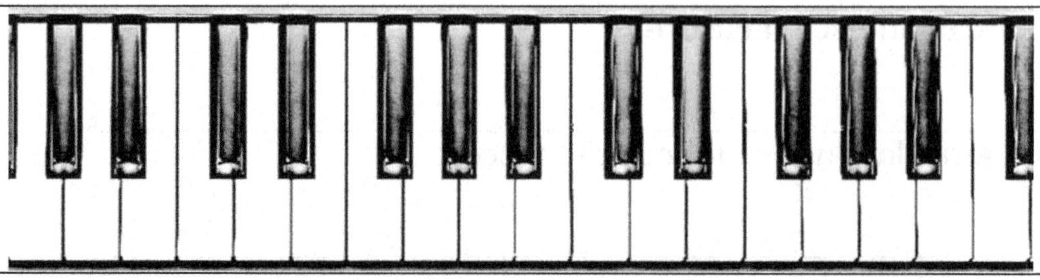

Guided Study: At First, Everything Is Difficult

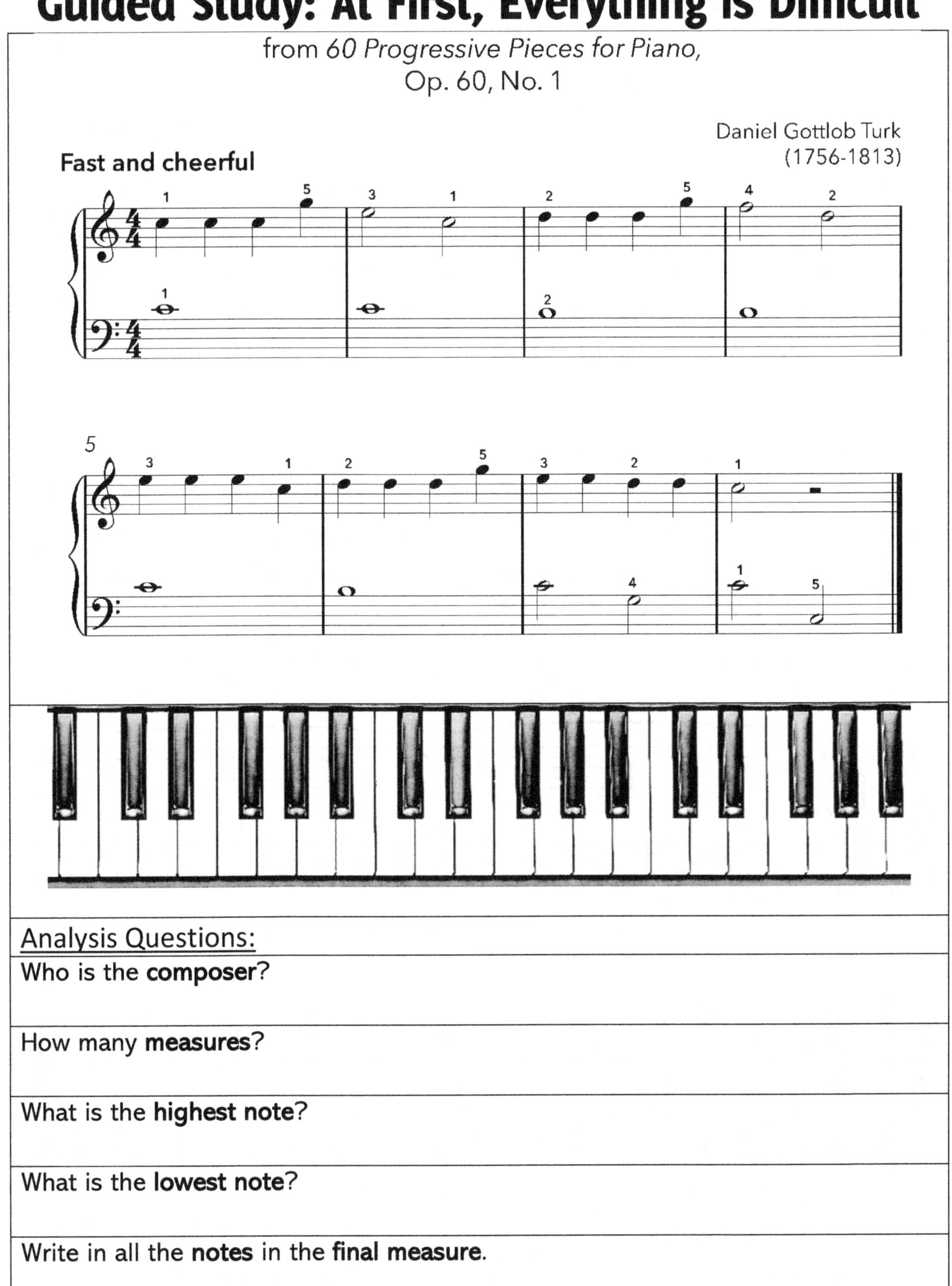

Analysis Questions:

Who is the **composer**?

How many **measures**?

What is the **highest note**?

What is the **lowest note**?

Write in all the **notes** in the **final measure**.

Guided Study: Song in C Major

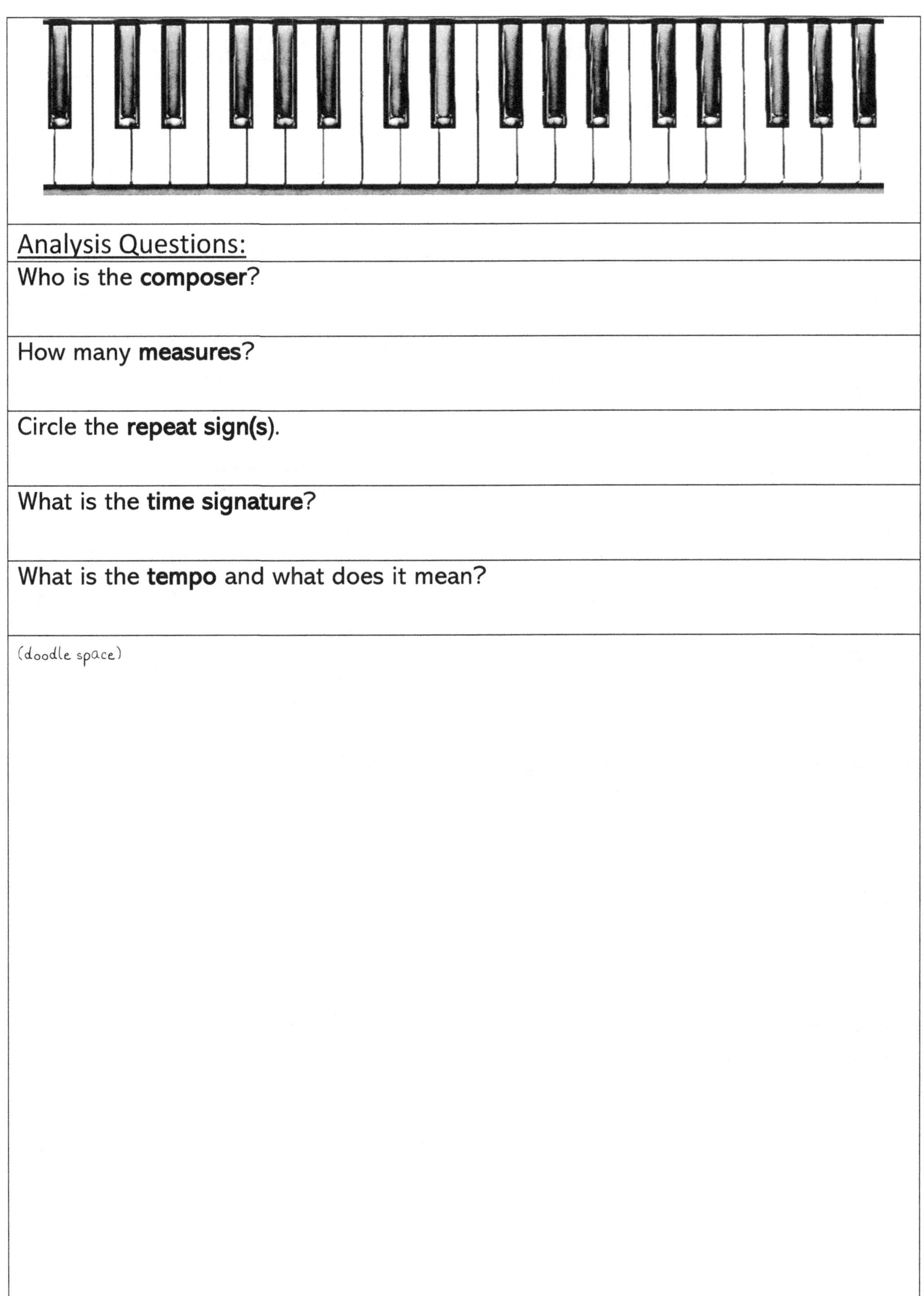

Analysis Questions:

Who is the **composer**?

How many **measures**?

Circle the **repeat sign(s)**.

What is the **time signature**?

What is the **tempo** and what does it mean?

(doodle space)

Guided Study: Etude in Staccato

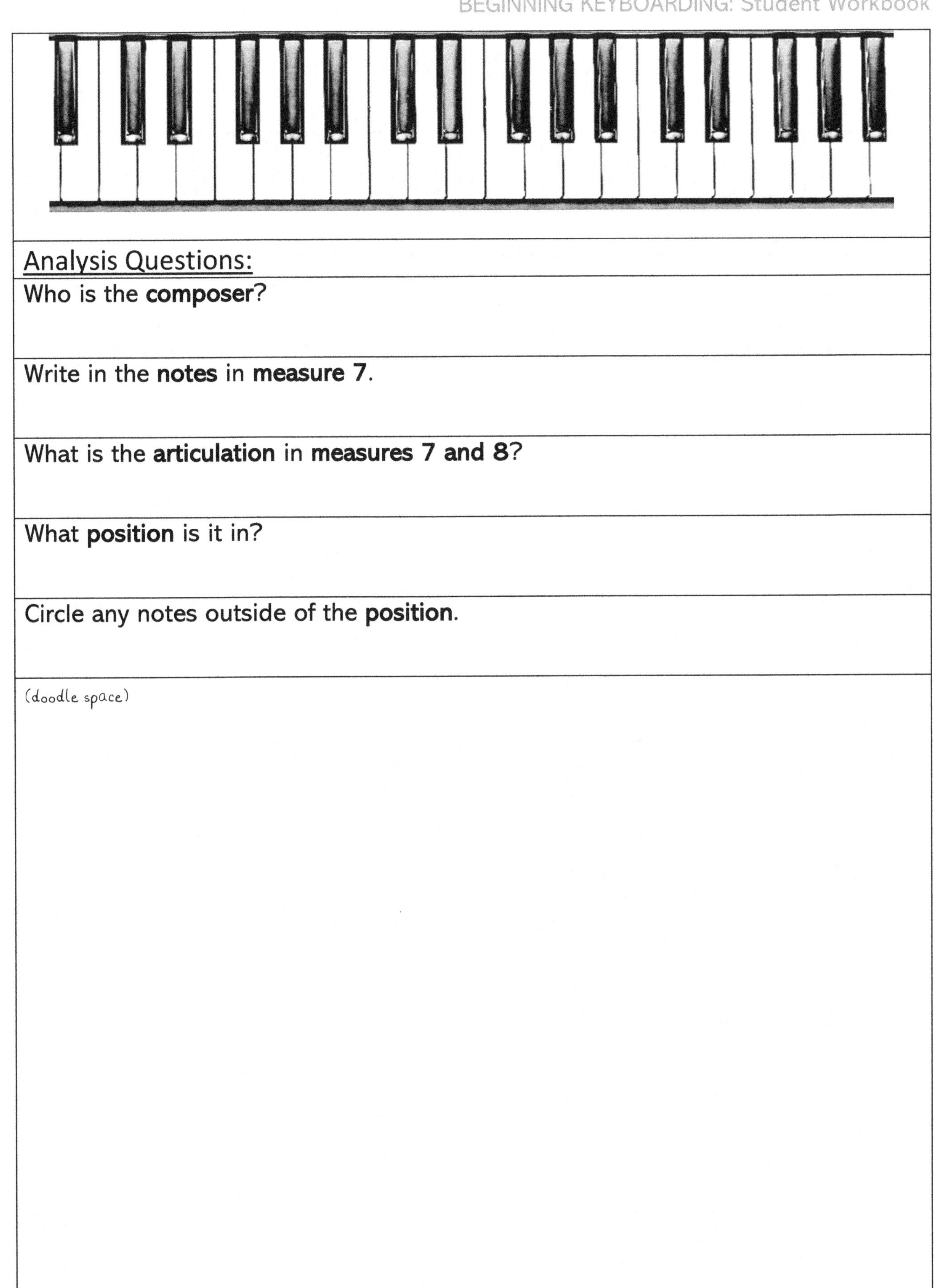

Analysis Questions:

Who is the **composer**?

Write in the **notes** in **measure 7**.

What is the **articulation** in **measures 7 and 8**?

What **position** is it in?

Circle any notes outside of the **position**.

(doodle space)

Position Workout

Positions:

Workout Chart:

Exercise Description	Score/Notes

Critical Viewing: Virtuoso Performance

Take notes while viewing a virtuoso performance. Use the questions below to guide your analysis.
Expression and Stage Presence: How did the pianist's expression and stage presence enhance the emotional impact of the music? Identify key moments where the performer's interpretation stood out to you and explain why.
Technique: What specific piano techniques did the virtuoso pianist employ during the performance, and how did these techniques contribute to the overall virtuosity of the piece?
Inspiration: Reflect on how the virtuoso's performance might inspire you in your own piano playing. Are there specific aspects of their technique or musical expression that you would like to incorporate into your practice?
Interpretation: How would you describe the performer's interpretation of the piece? Discuss the unique qualities and choices that made this performance stand out to you.
Overall Impressions:

Composers, Arrangers, and Publishers

Composers:
Arrangers:
Publishers:
Analysis Questions:
What **position** is the song in?
What is the **time signature**?
What **chord** is being played in **measure 2** (including both hands)?
Write in the notes in **measure 8** (in both hands).
What kind of note is counted for the **beat**?

The Itsy Bitsy Spider
Traditional
arr. Sidewalk Labs
The it - sy bit - sy spi - der climbed up the wat - er spout.
Down came the rain and washed the spi - der out.
Out came the sun and dried up all the rain, And the
it - sy bit - sy spi - der climbed up the spout a - gain.

Intervals

Half Steps:

Whole Steps:

Post Questions:
Name two notes that are a **half step** apart.
Name two notes that are a **whole step** apart.
If keys on the keyboard are **two whole steps** apart, how many keys separate them?
What note is a **half step** above "C"?
What note is a **whole step** below "C"?
(doodle space)

Guided Study: Jingle Bells

Analysis Questions:
Who is the composer?
What position is it in?
How many measures contain whole notes?
The word “jingle” always starts on what note in the melody?
What is the tempo?
(doodle space)

Guided Study: Legato in G Major

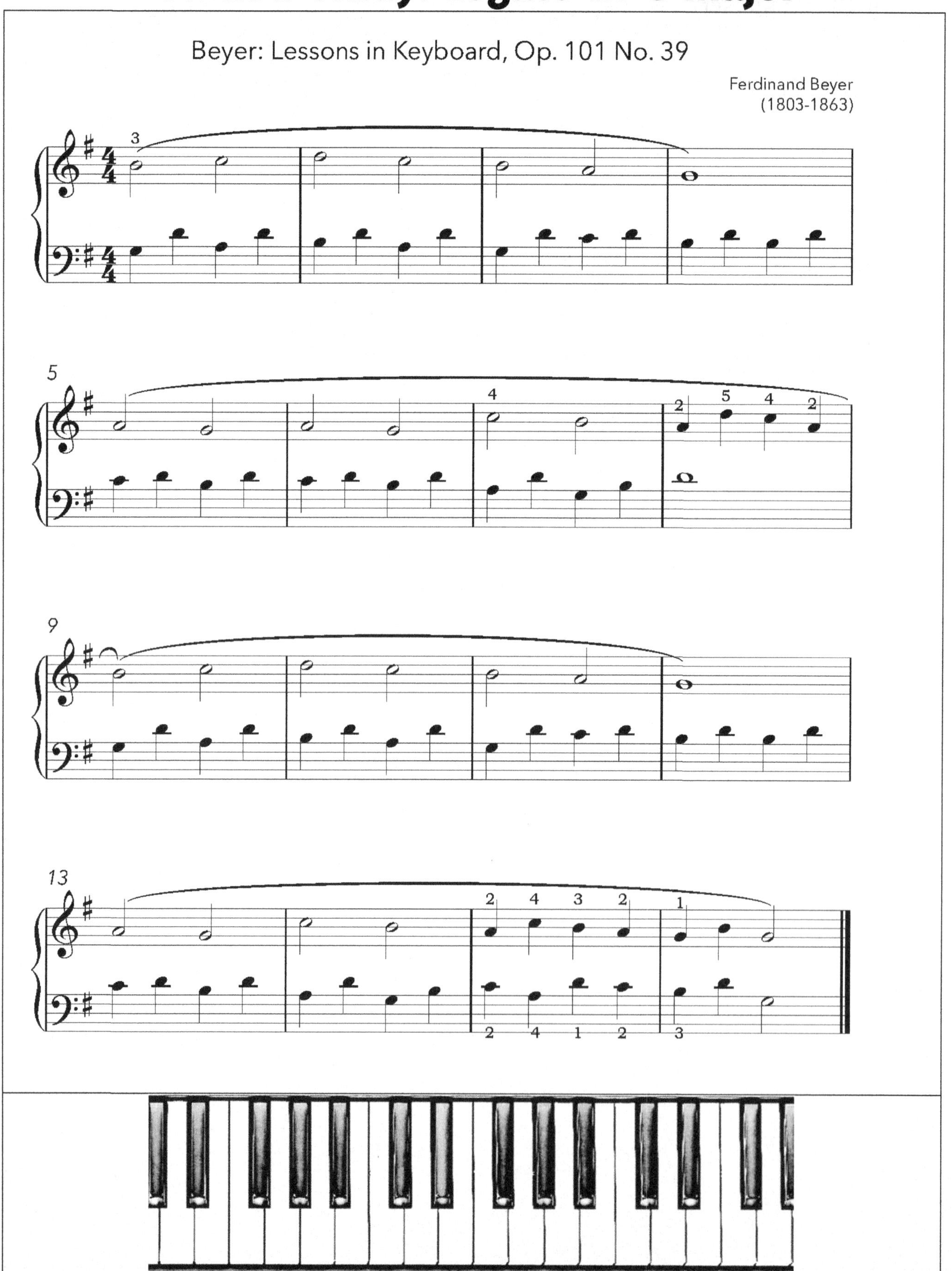

Analysis Questions:
What year was the **composer** born?
Write in all the **finger numbers** for **measures 1 and 2**, using **G position**.
What is the **interval** between the first two notes in the right hand?
Write in the **notes** in both hands in measure 5.
What is the **articulation** in the right hand?
(doodle space)

Listening for Shapes in Music

The following phrases will be presented out of order. Try to identify the correct order in which you hear them. Look them over before the beginning of the presentation and see if you can imagine any aspect of their sound.

Level 2: Scaling the Keys

Register Change:

C Major Scale:

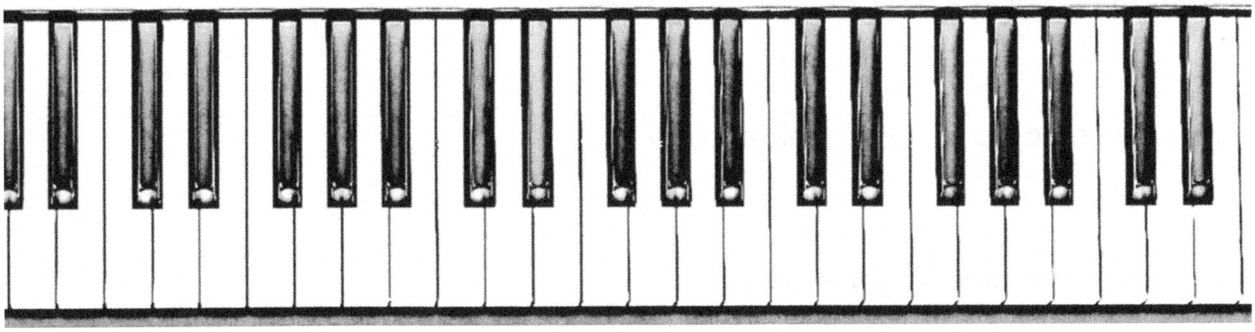

Scaling the Keys

Analysis Questions:

How many **measures**?

What is the **highest note** in the piece?

At what **measure(s)** is there a **register change**?

What are the **notes** of the **C major scale**?

How many times do you play **middle C**?

Guided Study: Chord Etude

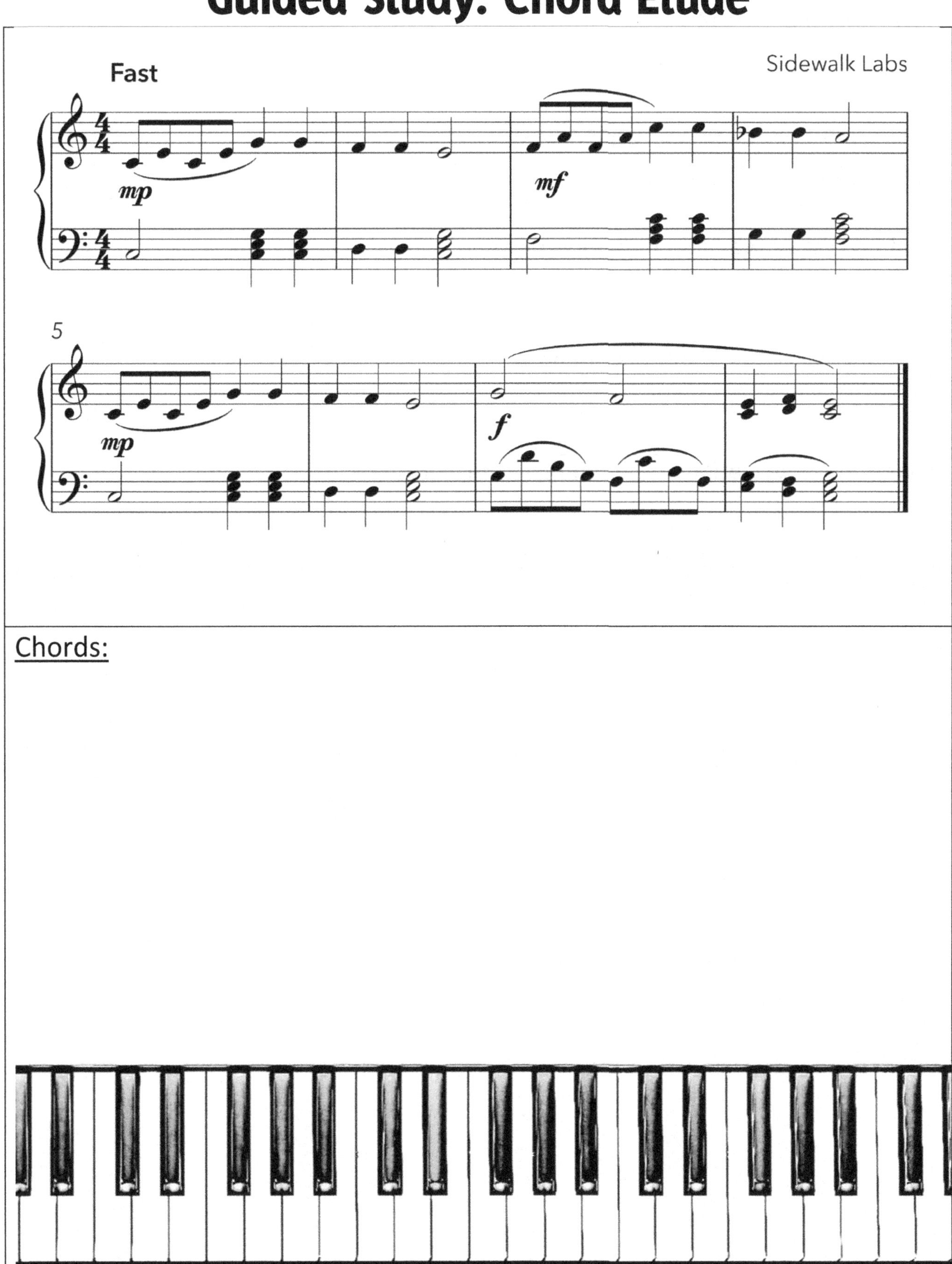

Analysis Questions:
How many **measures**?
What are the **notes** of a **C major chord**?
What are the **notes** of an **F major chord**?
What are the **notes** of a **G major chord**?
What is the **articulation** in the **final two measures**?
(doodle space)

Crossing Over

Octave Numbers:

Crossing Over:

Triplets:

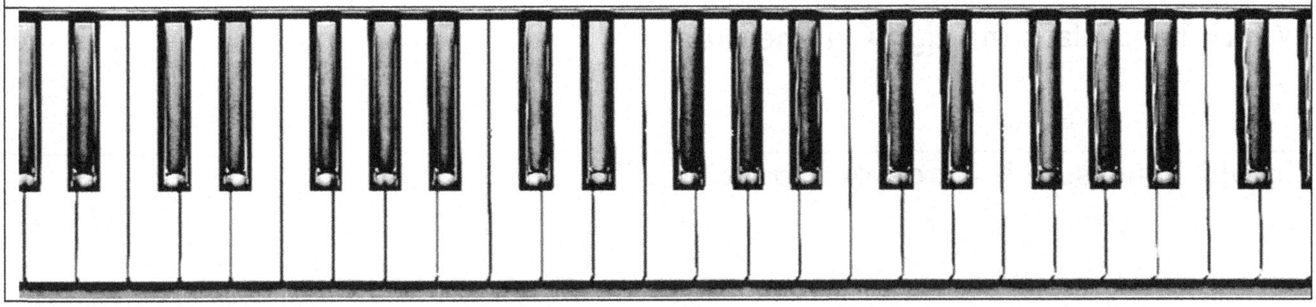

Row, Row, Row Your Boat

Traditional

Analysis Questions:

What is the **position**?

Circle a set of **triplets**.

Draw a box around a **dotted 8th note**.

Which hand plays the **high C** in measure 3?

In which measure is a **crossover** performed?

Guided Study: Amazing Grace

Analysis Questions:
How many **measures**?
What is the **position**?
What does the **time signature** say?
Does the piece contain **slurs**, **ties**, or both?
What is the **chord** in **measure 15** (including both hands)?
What is the **chord** in **measure 16** (including both hands)?
(doodle space)

Major Scales

Scales:

The Major Scale:

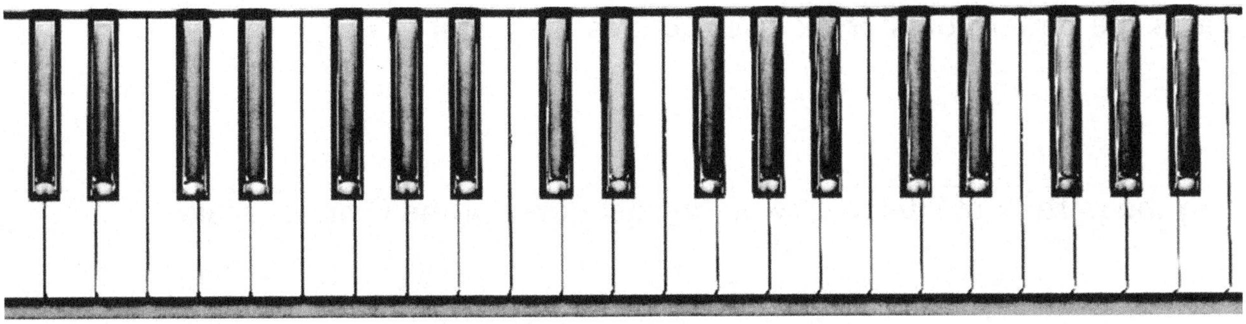

The C Major Scale:

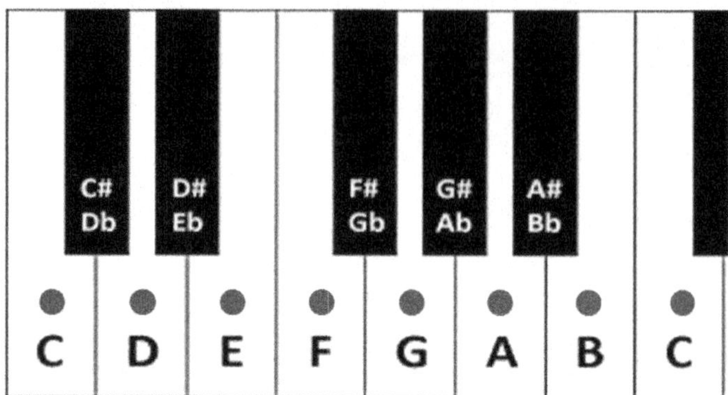

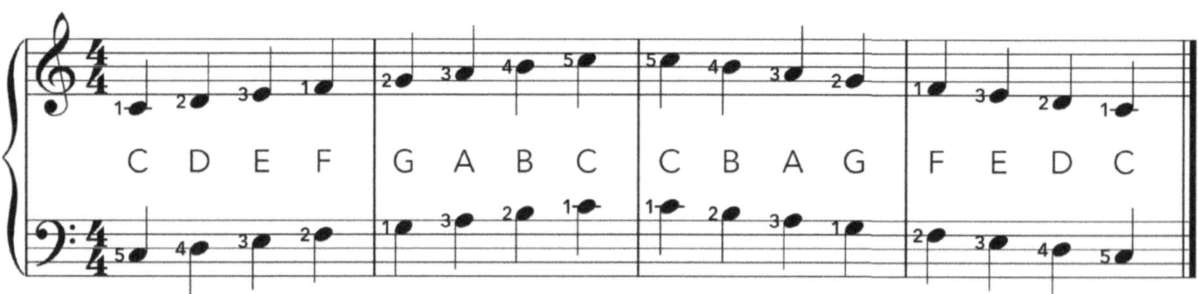

Post Questions:

Major scales have what type of mood or **quality**?

What is the pattern of **intervals** used to create a **major scale**?

Using the pattern of intervals, work out the notes of the **G major scale**.

Minor Scales

Review:

The Minor Scale:

Intervals of a Minor Scale:

Post Questions:
How many different types of **minor scales** are frequently used?
Which type of **minor scale** did we work on today?
Which **natural minor scale** uses no black keys on the keyboard?
Identify the correct keys for ***C natural minor scale.*** 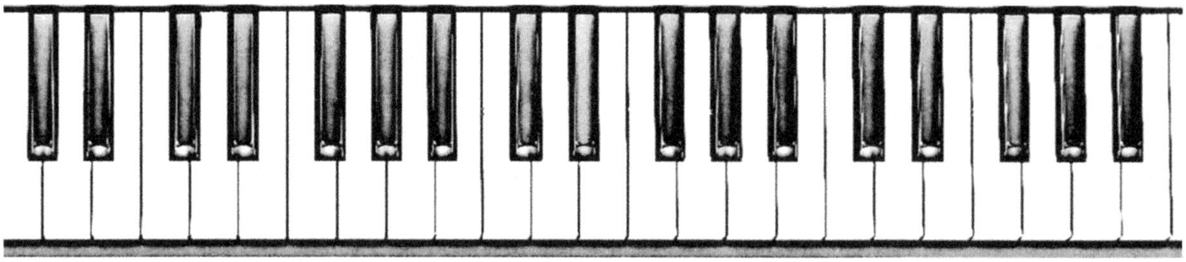
(doodle space)

Listening: Major vs Minor

<table>
<tr><td colspan="2">Scales Review:</td></tr>
<tr><td colspan="2">Transpositions and Mode Changes:</td></tr>
<tr><td rowspan="12">Identify the scale by listening.</td><td>1</td></tr>
<tr><td>2</td></tr>
<tr><td>3</td></tr>
<tr><td>4</td></tr>
<tr><td>5</td></tr>
<tr><td>6</td></tr>
<tr><td>7</td></tr>
<tr><td>8</td></tr>
<tr><td>9</td></tr>
<tr><td>10</td></tr>
<tr><td>11</td></tr>
<tr><td>12</td></tr>
</table>

w l e n t o r h y t h m g l x m a e d y r t

e n i a c y e l e e e m j p f r v i o q a d

k k o a e f i n g e r s x n a a c w d n q u

s n o i t i t e p m o c j i t l d k n g o o

y s t y l f r f m i d s e c a k y o a u m y

g g t y y s n m e z z o o s n o n c s l i e

p n e u i e y r c o r z s x o d a s s t s c

z i r e m r l w u d u i i r i n m c i n s i

o p g t p i j b i n c e f r t e i a l e i t

o m e r r t q a e a u o c f a u c l g m n c

g o l o o a s a l r y u u n i n s e n a a a

m c l f v r e u b e t o w u a i d u p n i r

p p a e i d o u y l d c t i b m i f y r p p

e d o d s a y e r e d o y a h i r b f o s t

d u d s a n y i i c u b m j r d e o f w y e

a t s s t d x a o c z e g n l e t j f n a u

l t y a i o x l e a s v a v o p d c e r e o

e v e b o o r e c i t a l k m x r o n y e w

n a k e n d y y r o i g g e p r a o m u i p

pianissimo accelerando competition performance diminuendo improvisation
rhythm practice octave treble classical comping recital mezzo fingers
glissando ornament dynamics arpeggio allegretto ritardando moderato
forte keys bass riff lento pedal scale

(doodle space)

Finding the Key

<u>Runs:</u>
<u>The "Tonic":</u>
<u>Identifying the Key:</u>

Post Questions:

Where in the music are you most likely to find the **tonic**?

How many **keys** exist for each **key signature**?

Build the **D major scale**.

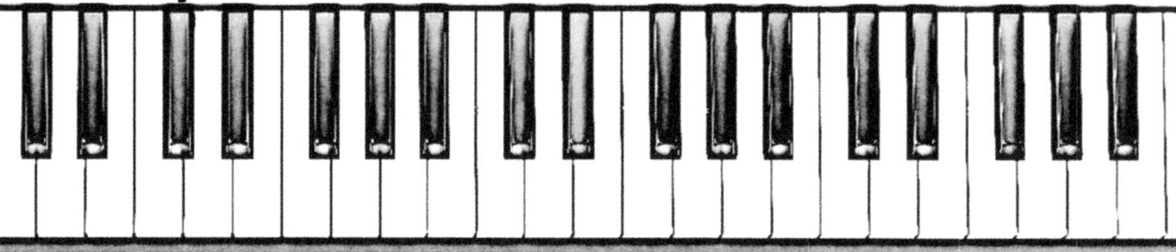

Build the **G natural minor scale**.

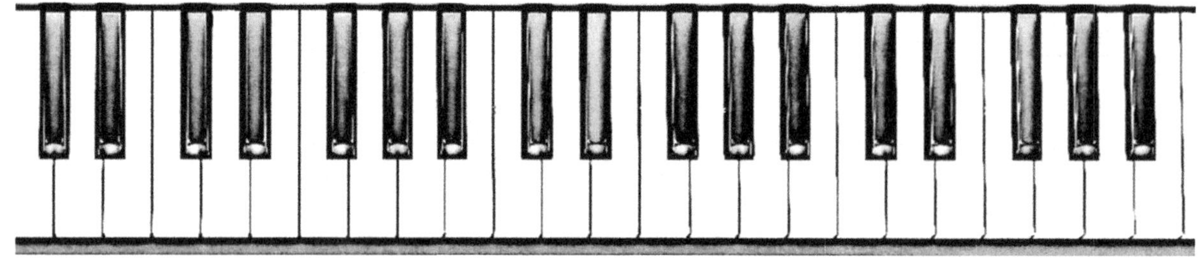

Key Signatures - Treble Clef

Key Signatures - Bass Clef

Transposition

Transposing:

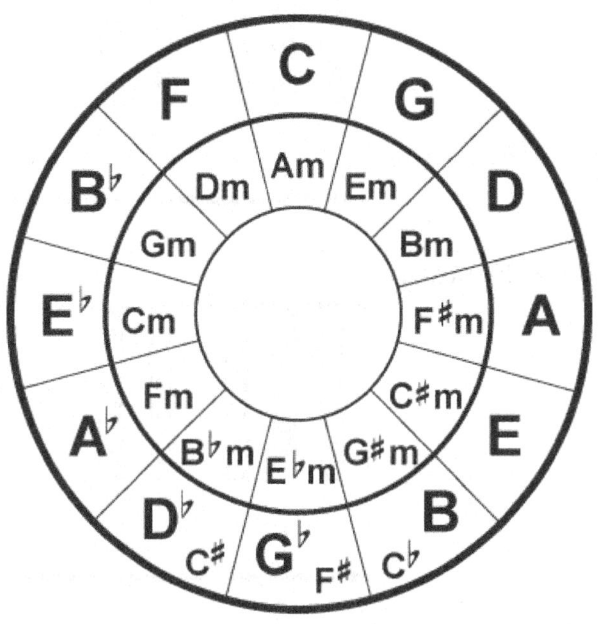

Transposable Repertoire:

Transposition By Position:

Original Position
New Position:

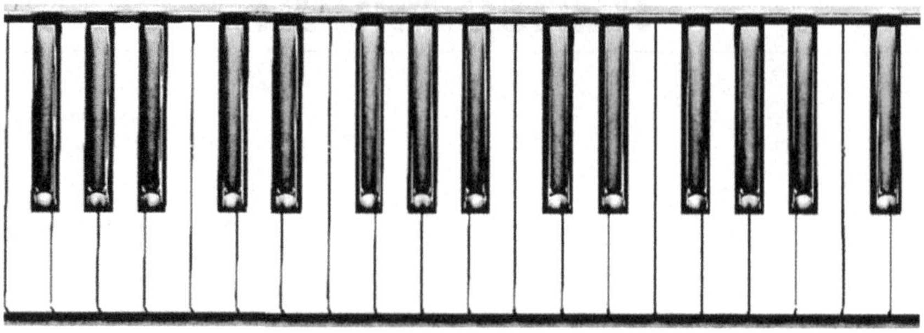

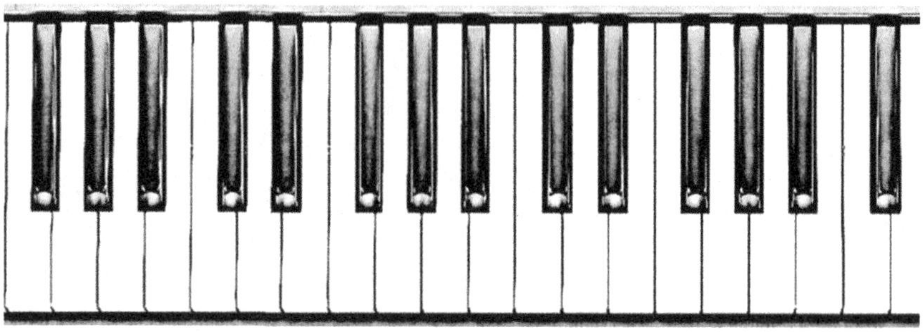

Post Questions:
When a piece has been **transposed**, what has changed about it?
What are the notes of **C major position**?
What are the notes of **G major position**?
Try moving the **C major position** song on the next page into **G major position.**
(doodle space)

Guided Study: Allegretto in C Major

Analysis Questions:
Who is the **composer**?
Write in the **notes** in **measure 7.**
When you reach the end, you should **repeat** back to which **measure**?
What is the **articulation** in right hand?
What is the **time signature**?
(doodle space)

The Key of G Major

Review:

G Major Scale:

Post Questions:
How many **black keys** appear in the key of **G major**, and which are they?
A **key signature** with an **F#** in it indicates one of which two possible keys?
In the following song, write in the notes in measure 3.

A Man Without Worry

from *60 Progressive Pieces for Piano,*
Op. 60, No. 4

Daniel Gottlob Turk
(1756-1813)

5

Transposition by Substitution

Review:

Scale Substitution:

Scale 1: _____ _____ _____ _____ _____ _____ _____

Scale 2: _____ _____ _____ _____ _____ _____ _____

This Old Man

TRANSPOSITION CROSSWORD

Across:

2. The circle of ___________ is used by musicians to see common musical relationships.
8. A five-note scale.
9. To ____________ means to move a piece from one key to another.
10. The underlying set of notes that a piece is built on, e.g. "D Major."
11. The notes of a key presented in sequence, frequently practiced as an exercise.

Down:

1. The key or scale that traditionally is considered to sound serious or sad.
3. The number of major and minor keys, or the number of notes in the chromatic scale.
4. A note adjusted to a slightly lower pitch; the symbol to adjust a note lower by a half-step.
5. The key or scale that is traditionally considered to sound happy.
6. A medieval form of scale; another word for scale.
7. A sharp, flat, or natural that is not a part of the key signature.
11. A note adjusted to a slightly higher pitch; the symbol to adjust a note higher by a half-step.

From C Major to G Major

Transposition Review:

Substitution:

Scale 1: _____ _____ _____ _____ _____ _____ _____

Scale 2: _____ _____ _____ _____ _____ _____ _____

Position:

Original Position

New Position:

Lavender's Blue

English Folk Song

Gently

From A minor to E minor

Minor Keys Review:

Substitution:

Scale 1: _____ _____ _____ _____ _____ _____ _____

Scale 2: _____ _____ _____ _____ _____ _____ _____

Position:

Original Position

New Position:

Snake Charmer

Traditional

What **key** is the song in?
What is the **articulation** in the right hand?
What is the **articulation** in the left hand?
Write all the **notes** in the **final measure**, including both hands.
Circle a **diminuendo**.

Transposition vs Mode Change

Elements of a "Key:"
Transposition:
Mode Change:
Additional Types of Scales and Keys:
What are the two essential parts of naming a **key**?
When performing a **transposition**, which aspect of the key has changed?
When performing a **mode change**, which aspect of the key has changed?

Scale Workout

Scale(s):

Workout Chart:

Exercise Description	Score/Notes

Intervals Review

Half Steps:

Whole Steps:

Sharps and Double Sharps:

Flats and Double Flats:

Scale Intervals

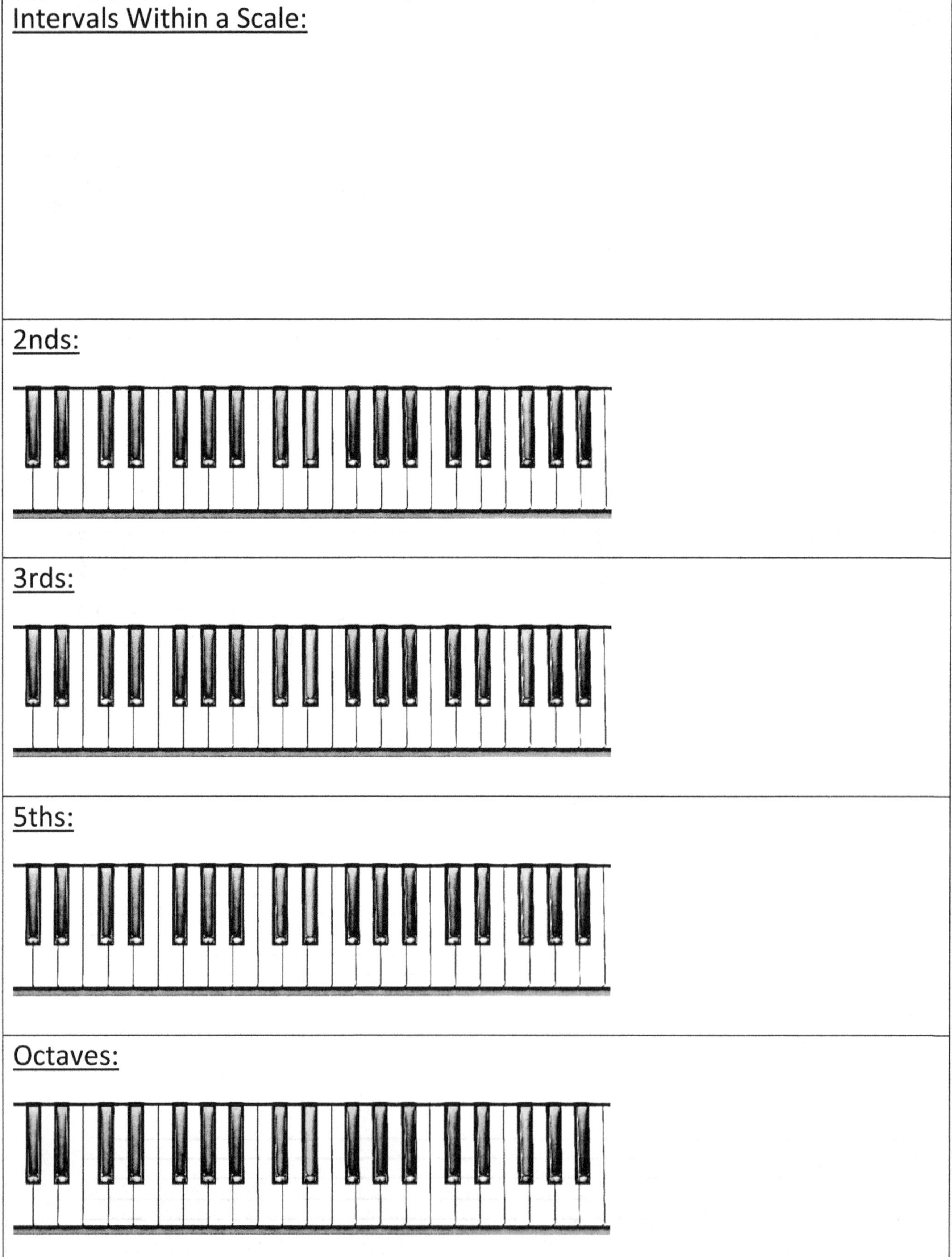

Reading and Playing Intervals

Intervals on a Staff:

2nds:

3rds:

5ths:

Octaves:

Chord Workout

Chord(s):

Workout Chart:

Exercise Description	**Score/Notes**

Relative Keys

Relative Keys:

G major:

E minor:

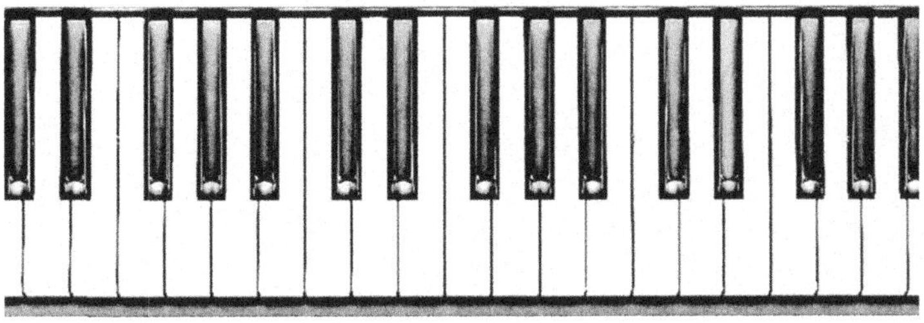

Post Questions:
Two keys that are **relatives** have what in common?
What is the **relative major** of **E minor**?
Which **black key** is included in both **E minor** and **G major**?
Write the notes to the **G major scale**:
Write the notes to the **E minor scale**:
(doodle space)

Parallel Keys

Parallel Keys:

C major:

C minor:

Post Questions:
Two keys that are **parallel** have what in common?
What is the **parallel major** of **C minor**?
Write the notes to the **C major scale**:
Write the notes to the **C minor scale**:
(doodle space)

Circle of Fifths

Circle of Fifths:

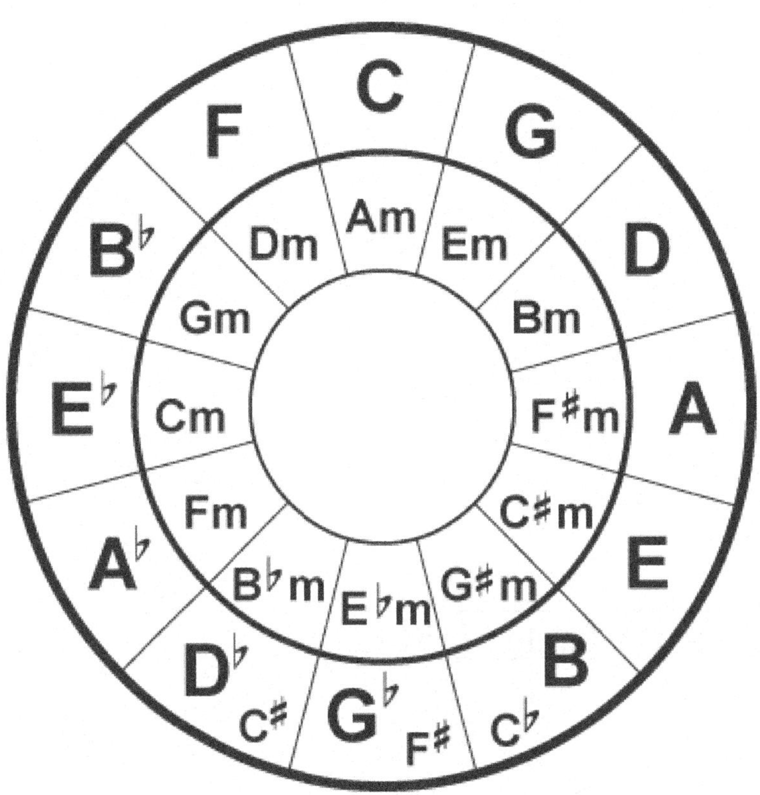

Relationships Between Keys:

Key Signatures:

Using the Circle of Fifths:

How can the Circle of Fifths help you determine the relative minor of a major key or the relative major of a minor key?

When playing the piano, if a song is in the key of C major, what would be the key that is one position clockwise on the Circle of Fifths? What about one position counterclockwise?

Chord Workout

Chord(s):

Workout Chart:

Exercise Description	Score/Notes

Building a Circle of Fifths

Process:
Circle:

Additional Markings:

How many **half steps** between each clockwise turn of the circle?

Which side of the circle contains **sharp key signatures**?

Which side of the circle contains **flat key signatures**?

(doodle space)

Common Keys by Level

Equivalency of Keys:
Level 1 Keys:
Level 2 Keys:
Level 3 Keys:
Level 4+:

Fluency of Keys

Language of Music:

Keys in Translation:

Understanding Repertoire:

Scale Workout

Scale(s):

Workout Chart:

Exercise Description	Score/Notes

Baroque Period

Western Music Tradition:
Baroque Period:
Post Questions:
How long ago did the **western music tradition** begin?
What years does the period known as the **Baroque** cover?
What are two common characteristics of **Baroque music**?

Y H Q E R A G F X E A Y E C N A G E L E
T R W N G K T J K U W T K K W V X O E G
B A R O Q U E A Y I E I Y C L N W R Z D
I N S T R U M E N T S L A X A Z M N D F
S U I T E W K G C O N A P G H R Z A H A
Y L D F P V H I T Z S N R G A E L M R Y
H N A T A T N A C L K O X U N P P E R M
Y A O P W N A L E W I T A E D R P N W O
I A R H C Y C P P H Q T F E E O O T S J
S D W P P O G Y I V A U J L L G I A T K
G M L A S Y N S P C G I U J T A H T R J
B O H A I I L C C U L D A H P G C I I I
S V P L V J C O E C E Z T K Z L A O N E
Z K N E M I T H P R X J L W H E B N G D
V H Y X Q D V S O C T Y W E H F W K S M
R K F G J B K E E R J O B C D P U P J J
T Q C Q H W V M N U D M K W J T L Z L D
T N I O P R E T N U O C U Y P E U U H A
O M F K F B F P V D M F Q X F B Q L N P
V Z Q N G O T T U O U I J P O F C L Z G

Bach
Baroque
cantata
concerto
counterpoint
elegance

fancy
fugue
Handel
harpsichord
instruments
opera

organ
ornamentation
pipe
polyphony
prelude
sonata

strings
suite
toccata
tonality
Vivaldi

(doodle space)

Antonio Vivaldi

Antonio Vivaldi:

Mandolin Concerto in C Major:

Post Questions:

What was **Vivaldi's** nickname and why was he called by it?

What does it mean to be a **virtuoso**?

What were your overall impressions of this piece?

Mandolin Concerto in C Major

Allegro Theme

Johann Sebastian Bach

<u>J.S. Bach:</u>

<u>Air on the G String:</u>

<u>Post Questions:</u>

What **instrument** was **Bach** famous in his day for his **virtuosic** ability to play?

The **melody** was intended to be played on just one string of which **instrument**?

What were your overall impressions of this piece?

Air on the G String

JS Bach (1685-1750)

George Frideric Handel

Handel:
Music for the Royal Fireworks:
Post Question:
Name one thing Bach and Handel had in common.
In which country did Handel live most of his life?
Which was your favorite of the Baroque composers and why?

Minuet No. 1

from *Music for the Royal Fireworks*

Classical Period

History Review:

The Classical Period:

Post Questions:

What aspects of the **Baroque Period** did the **Classical Period** reject?

What years does the **period** known as the **classical** cover?

What are two common characteristics of **classical music**?

V Y K Q L X N E A A H R M N I N E K T B
W G T W D O G L W B R W W D D C C Z N M
R T W T O Z N E I F C P R Y Q K N Y E B
M U R S U L U G H D X V A W O E A J M W
P E S E O Y R A Y N O H P M Y S L I I O
S A L L B W Y N M C L A S S I C A L N O
B M J O V U A C S U E V F D Y T B B A D
V P U S D M H E P G S N W M Z Z N H P W
N F P X I Y H C Q P N Q N Q K E D S M I
N U Z C T M R O S Q N C H R V V I J O N
I T S G R Q P S A F X D Z O O C M C C D
V N K D A K G L L T J Y H Z K H E X C S
W D A D Z A U I I J R T O N A I P N A C
Y O D P O Z G R A C E F U L N E S S Q L
A A C C M H R I V E I T X B Z V Z P I E
T Y O P T I S Y B L U T X C G A A W D M
J R F N X B T E Y P Z I Y M L N X I H E
F Y E P T C N J L H R O T W M G T N X N
Q S S C N N G Z F O R M S U A A O A N T
S C R X G S J T N V D G A L O L Q R H I

accompaniment
balance
bassoon
Beethoven
classical
Clementi
dynamics
elegance
form
gracefulness
Haydn
horn
lightness
melody
Mozart
piano
Schubert
simplicity
symphony
timpani
woodwinds

(doodle space)

Franz Josef Haydn

Haydn:
Emperor's Hymn:
Post Questions:
What affectionate nickname did **Mozart** call **Haydn** that is still used?
What **instruments** are included in a **string quartet**?
What two things was **Haydn** known as the "Father of"?

Andante Theme from

Surprise Symphony

from Symphony No. 94, 2nd Movement

Wolfgang Amadeus Mozart

<u>Mozart:</u>

<u>Eine Kleine Nachtmusik:</u>

<u>Post Questions:</u>

What does it mean to be a **prodigy**?

How old was **Mozart** when he died?

Allegro Theme from

A Little Night Music

from Serenade No. 13 (*Eine Kleine Nachtmusik*),
1st Movement

Wolfgang Amadeus Mozart
(1776-1791)

Allegro

f

5

mp

9

p

13

opt. 8vb

17

(8)

f

Ludwig van Beethoven

Beethoven:

Fur Elise:
Post Questions:
In what European city did the three **classical composers** establish their reputations?
How is Beethoven's personality and later music considered "**Romantic**?"
How long after Beethoven died was Fur Elise published?

Fur Elise
Bagatelle No. 25 in A minor, WoO 59
Ludwig van Beethoven
(1770-1827)
very graceful, with motion
pp
6
10
mp
p
15
19
rit.

Early Romantic Period

History Review:
The Romantic Period:
The Early Romantic Period:
Post Questions:
What aspects of the **Classical Period** did the **Romantic Period** reject?
What years does the **period** known as the **Romantic** cover?
Why is the Romantic divided into early and late periods?

N I Y G C K B T D E M C J K H O T K Z Q
C T N C U R R Z X E E I W A W L S J W S
R O N M A E L P N S R T N N T Y I C G T
S E T B B P R D E B J A Z D H A E S T O
L E C U K E E I Y G N M C N J A N T Z R
U N H P S L N U N B N M B E R L I O Z T
Y C U S S O J X Y E F A P I K O K U S I
S X I S H W U M K H C R G J Y A N R E Q
K O O P T I J O W S Z G N K Y N A C D T
N H M I F A F R D Q S O Q F O E T E A S
N Y O W K R F Q Y N V R R K I V I A L C
S O M O S O U T R I V P S L A O O P L H
R Q R P G P C X X E V X L W D H N F A U
R U E C S H Q T Y G D F A P K T A Y B M
W G J X H D I A A U O E Q P S E L A L A
N J B R K E U H J L T Z I H F E I I I N
W H P T O H S W K N W L Z L X B S H T N
Y G E L E B D T P J Y D O L E M M V W H
Y W X L V A T Z R F W E G J T N X S U Z
P I A N O W Z D H A A B O I J C A F C L

ballade
Beethoven
Berlioz
elegy
expression
folk
lieder

Liszt
melody
Mendelssohn
nationalism
orchestra
piano
programmatic

Schubert
Schumann
sonata
song
symphonies
virtuoso

(doodle space)

Franz Schubert

Schubert:

Piano Trio in E-Flat:
Post Questions:
How many concerts of his works did Schubert give in his lifetime?
In what form of music did Schubert make his most indelible mark and compose his greatest amount of work?
How old was Schubert when he died?

Andante Theme

from *Piano Trio in E-flat*

Frederic Chopin

Chopin:
Nocturnes:
Post Questions:
What **instrument** did **Chopin** compose almost exclusively for?
Where did **Chopin** prefer to perform instead of in concert halls?
What does the word **nocturne** refer to?

Nocturne Op. 55, No. 1

Felix Mendelssohn

Mendelssohn:

A Midsummer Night's Dream:

Post Questions:

How old was Mendelssohn when his first work was published?

Which virtuoso was Mendelssohn often compared to at a young age?

Who wrote the play *A Midsummer Night's Dream* that Mendelssohn wrote incidental music for?

Nocturne

from *A Midsummer Night's Dream*

Felix Mendelssohn (1809-1847)

Late Romantic Period

History Review:
The Late Romantic Period:
Post Questions:
Name at least one instrument that got added to the **orchestra** in the late Romantic Period?
What is meant by the term **nationalism**?
Describe what is meant by "**Romanticism**" when referring to the music of this time period?

S H P F T Y D F V B Y N W T C B E N T O
Y D O L E M N P F K X A Y H K X V A D P
E E Q K N D E O S O G A R W P L I S Z T
M B O Z O H T V H N N O G R R W T O E M
O I J S T O O S E P M I E S S U A R T S
T D X J N K P R I A M S N N A K T J W R
I R N O I A J Z T F S Y X A P Z Q G I U
O E H A R U I I C I V Y S R M R Q T P H
N V H E T N C D O A R H W R B H C Q T H
Q C P P Y I A N K N L H M A G I C A J C
T O Q Y M N O G I I H E U T J R V A T C
L S P Y L O R N F O O J J I L O Z X R S
S U I L E B I S A P T Z Z V P O E F S S
B P A U D D P K E L H K Y E S T F V G K
E P W M Q Q V F J T I E Y P K R N S L G
V S Q A O P O O M K U S E F O E G U I C
B R A H M S D I R A B T T O N C H P F F
O I S L J O T D J A I J E I S N F S H P
K S P E N D R K G W K H O F C O H O U O
H X X R A M C Y K E Q Y Q C N C V T W L

Brahms
chromatic
concerto
Dvorak
emotion
expression
Liszt
lush
Mahler
melody
narrative
nationalistic
opera
poem
Rachmaninoff
Sibelius
Strauss
symphony
Tchaikovsky
tone
Verdi
Wagner

(doodle space)

Pyotr Ilyich Tchaikovsky

Tchaikovsky:

Swan Lake:

Post Questions:

What country's music did Tchaikovsky blend with European Romanticism to form his own **nationalistic** style?

What theatrical form is ***Swan Lake*** an example of?

Name another popular work of Tchaikovsky's that is still regularly performed today.

Swan Lake Theme

Pyotr Ilyich Tchaikovsky
1840-1893

Johannes Brahms

Brahms:

Cradle Song:

Post Questions:

What aspects of the classical style did Brahms admire?

Brahms is occasionally grouped as one of the "Three B's," which includes which other two famous composers?

Lullaby

Op. 49, No. 4

Johannes Brahms (1833-1897)

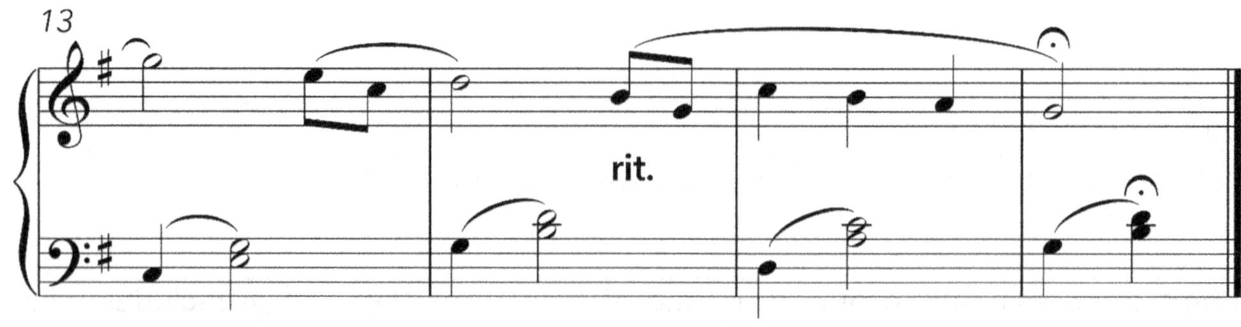

Edvard Grieg

Grieg:

Peer Gynt:

Post Questions:

In what country is Edvard Grieg considered a national hero?

What is meant by **program music**?

In the Hall of the Mountain King

adapted from *Peer Gynt Suite I*
Op. 46, No. 4

Edvard Grieg
1843-1907

Writing Notes

5-Layers Review:

Clefs:

Notes:

Writing Notes by Ear

2-Note Listening:

3-Note Listening:

4-Note Listening:

Writing Rhythms

5-Layers Review:

Note Decorations:

Rests:

Writing Rhythms by Ear

Quarters, Halfs and Wholes:

Add Rests:

Add Eighths and Dotted Notes:

Critical Listening: Virtuoso Performance

Take notes while listening to a virtuoso performance with provided sheet music. Use the questions below to guide your analysis.

Structure:

Many classical pieces have a specific structure or form (e.g., ABA, sonata form, rondo). As you listen, try to break down the piece into different sections based on changes in melody, rhythm, or mood. Can you label these sections in your sheet music?

Technique:

While listening, pay attention to the different piano techniques used by the pianist. Can you spot the ornamental trills, chord patterns, or rapid scale runs? Mark these on your sheet music. How do these techniques enhance the virtuosic nature of the piece?

Themes:

Can you identify the themes or melodies of the piece? Highlight or circle the sections in the sheet music where you hear different themes. How does the composer play around with them?

Interpretation:

How closely does the performer follow the dynamics and articulations listed in the sheet music? What seems unique or individual about their interpretation?

Overall Impressions:

Include a reflection on how having the sheet music affected your experience as a listener.

Writing Dynamics and Articulations

Italian Expressions:

Hairpins and Articulations:

Writing Notes and Rhythms by Ear

2-Note Listening:

3-Note Listening:

4-Note Listening:

Scale Workout

Scale(s):

Workout Chart:

Exercise Description	Score/Notes

Variations

Three Practice Pillars:

Melodic Variations:

Harmonic Variations:

Critical Listening: Theme and Variations

Take notes while listening to a virtuoso performance of a Theme and Variations by a master composer.
<u>Title and Composer:</u> Does it have a name other than "Theme and Variations?" Who wrote it?
<u>Tradition:</u> What period is it from? How does it represent that period's typical qualities?
<u>Themes:</u> Can you identify the theme or melody of the piece? Is the theme recognizable throughout the variations?
<u>Variations:</u> What are some of the things the composer does to vary the theme as the piece progresses? Try to describe your favorite variation.
<u>Overall Impressions:</u>

Melodic Variations

Variations on the Scale:

Identifying the Melody:

Melodic Variations

Register Changes and Doubling

Expanding the Musical Landscape with Register Changes:

Enriching Musical Texture with Doubling:

What symbol would you write in music to indicate a **register change**?

What interval can always be added to **double** effectively, no matter what?

What effect does a **register change** create?

How does **doubling** affect the sound of the melody?

Register Changes and Doubling in 'I Am So Weary and So Ill'

from 60 Progressive Pieces for Piano,
Op. 60, No. 9

Daniel Gottlob Türk
(1750-1813)

Largo molto e tenero

Number the **measures**.
Translate the **tempo**.
Circle the **repeat sign**.
What **key** is it in?
Name the **accidental(s)**.

Neighbor Notes and Passing Tones

Ornamentation with Neighbor Notes and Trills:

Connecting Dots with Passing Tones:

Draw the symbol for a **trill**.

What can you look for in a melody that creates an opportunity for a **neighbor note**?

What can you look for in a melody that creates an opportunity for a **passing tone**?

After adding a neighbor note or passing tone, what else must be adjusted to make up for it?

Neighbor Notes in the Tetris Theme

This Russian folk tune provided an excellent basis for a repetitive video game theme, as it lends itself – as much folk music does – to the use of common melodc variations. How long can you make it interesting? Try first applying neighbor notes and trills before moving to other creative melodic variations.

Listening for Melodic Variations

<table>
<tr><td colspan="2"><u>Variations Review:</u></td></tr>
<tr><td rowspan="12">Listen to each fragment played in its original form, then with a variation applied. Try to identify the variation used.</td><td>1.</td></tr>
<tr><td>2.</td></tr>
<tr><td>3.</td></tr>
<tr><td>4.</td></tr>
<tr><td>5.</td></tr>
<tr><td>6.</td></tr>
<tr><td>7.</td></tr>
<tr><td>8.</td></tr>
<tr><td>9.</td></tr>
<tr><td>10.</td></tr>
<tr><td>11.</td></tr>
<tr><td>12.</td></tr>
</table>

Melodic Variations Workout

Variation(s):

Workout Chart:

Exercise Description	**Score/Notes**

Study: Written Variations

Take any of the pieces that appear in this book and create a variation of the piece in the blank sheet below. Begin by making a direct copy of the music in pencil (so you can easily erase and replace). Make sure to leave enough space to add variations later. You will be graded using the rubric on the following page.

<u>Use of Variations (50 points):</u> At least six variations should appear, with at least three different types represented. Which type of variation should be obvious by context, or the variation should be labeled by name.	
<u>Musicality (30 points):</u> The variations should be musically appropriate, pleasant to the ear, and add to the character of the music. They should capture the correct notes, and not sound awkward or odd in playback.	
<u>Notation (20 points):</u> All variations should be notated properly, with necessary rhythmic adjustments, placement or removement of rests, note size and placement, and all other general notational elements should be followed.	
<u>FINAL GRADE:</u>	

Whole Tone Scale Workout

Whole Tone Scale(s):

Workout Chart:

Exercise Description	Score/Notes

Chromatic Scale Workout

Chromatic Scale:

Workout Chart:

Exercise Description	Score/Notes

Three Note Chord Workout

Chord(s):

Workout Chart:

Exercise Description	**Score/Notes**

Guided Study: Five-Note Sonatina

Analysis Questions:
Who is the composer and what period of music does he represent?
What key is it in?
What is the meaning of *poco rit.*? What measure does it appear in?
What feature of the music makes it easiest to play?
What two dynamics does it alternate between?
(doodle space)

Guided Study: The Cheerful Boy

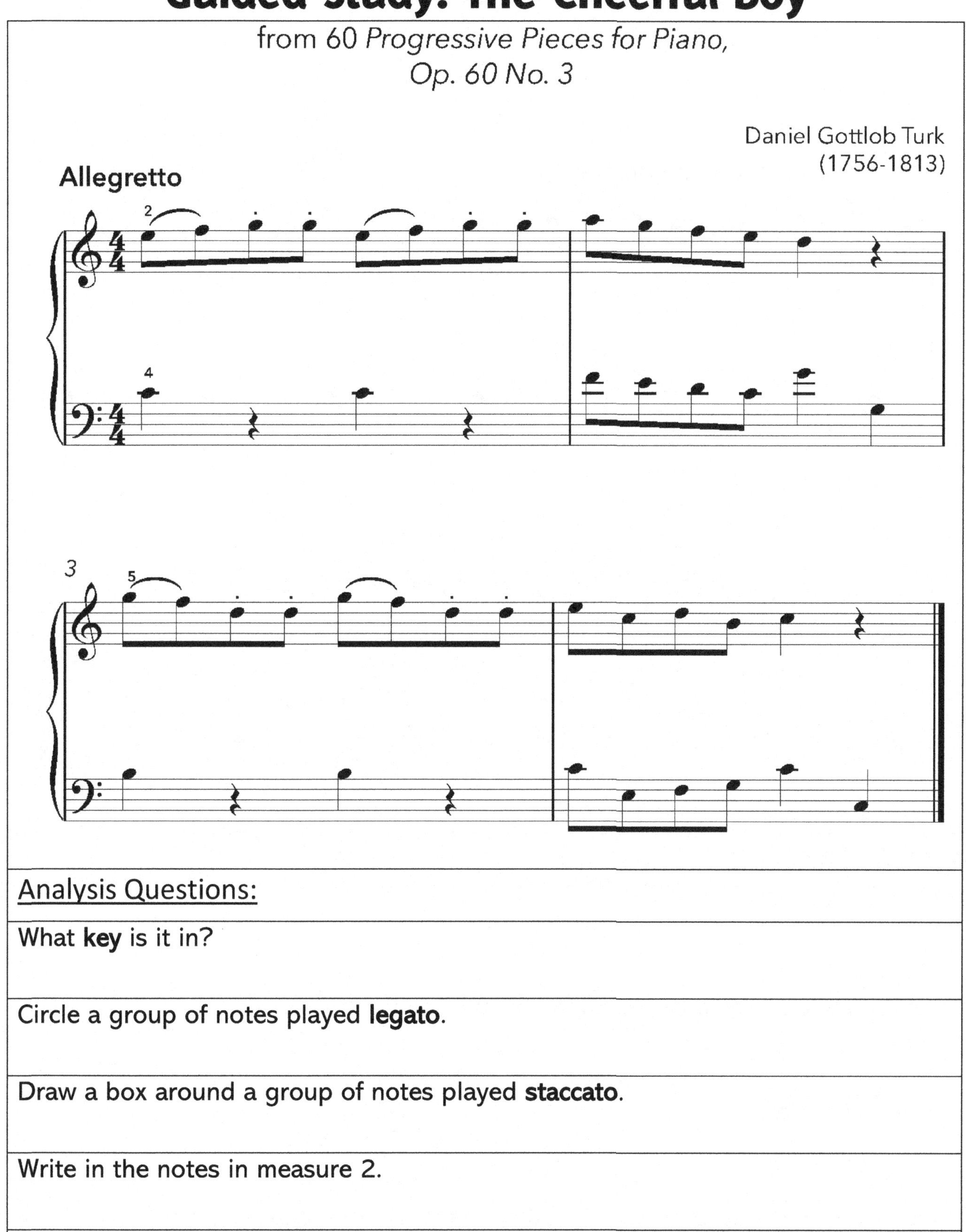

Analysis Questions:

What **key** is it in?

Circle a group of notes played **legato**.

Draw a box around a group of notes played **staccato**.

Write in the notes in measure 2.

Add at least one musically appropriate variation directly into the music.

Guided Study: Children's Song

from *60 Progressive Pieces for Piano,*
Op. 60, No. 11

Daniel Gottlob Turk
(1756-1813)

Andante con grazia

mf

Analysis Questions:

What key is it in?

What two notes should be alternated for the **trill**?

Write in the notes in measure 1.

Add at least one musically appropriate variation directly into the music.

Guided Study: Theme from "12 Variations on Ah! vous dirai-je, mam"

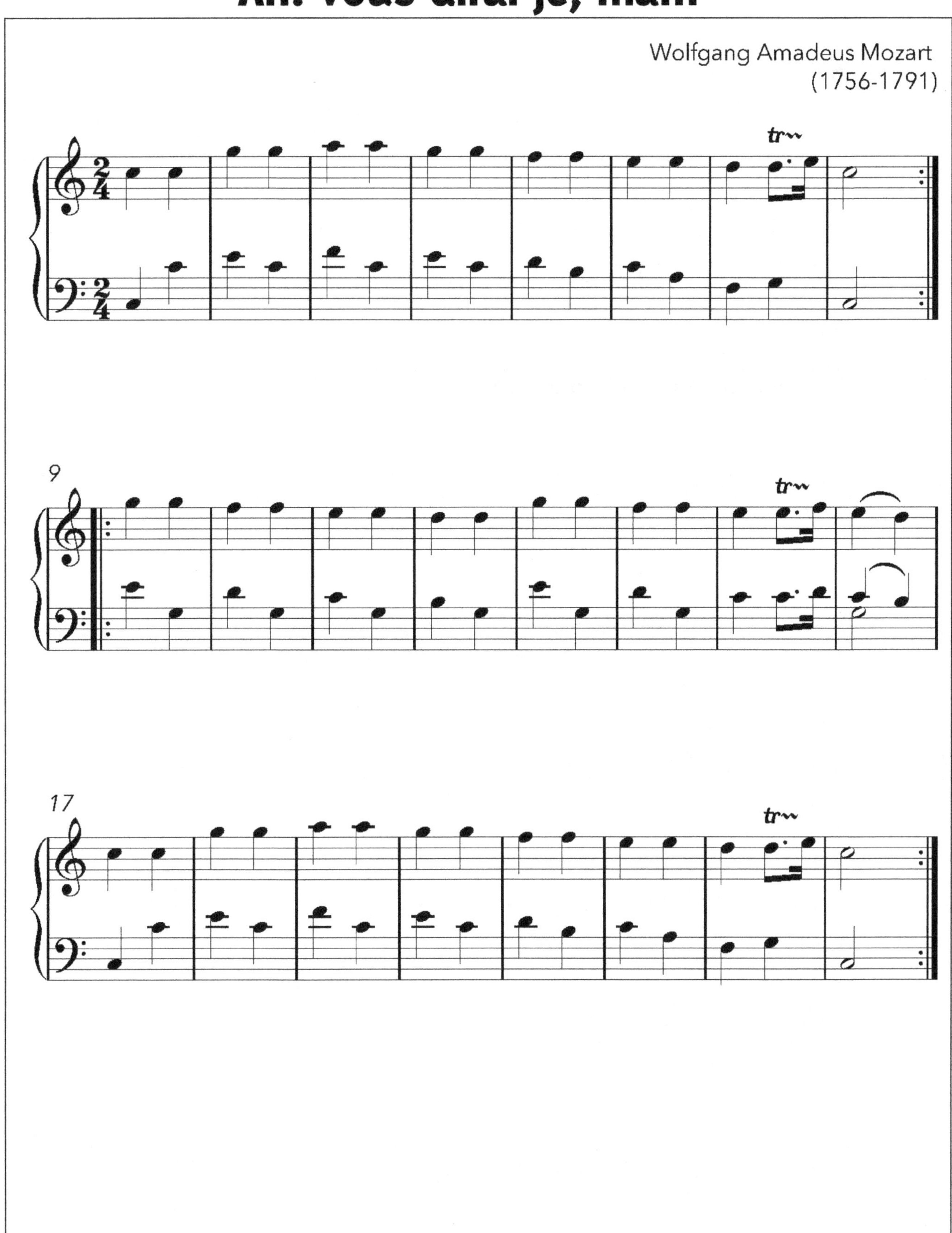

Analysis Questions:
Who is the composer and what period of music does he represent?
Circle a trill.
What key is it in?
Directly into the music, add at least one musically appropriate variation.
What is the common modern title or name of this piece?
(doodle space)

Guided Study: Spring

Analysis Questions:
Who is the composer and what period of music does he represent?
What key is it in?
Circle an instance of doubling.
Add at least one musically appropriate variation directly into the music.
What does the tempo say and what does it mean?
(doodle space)

Guided Study: Air from Water Music

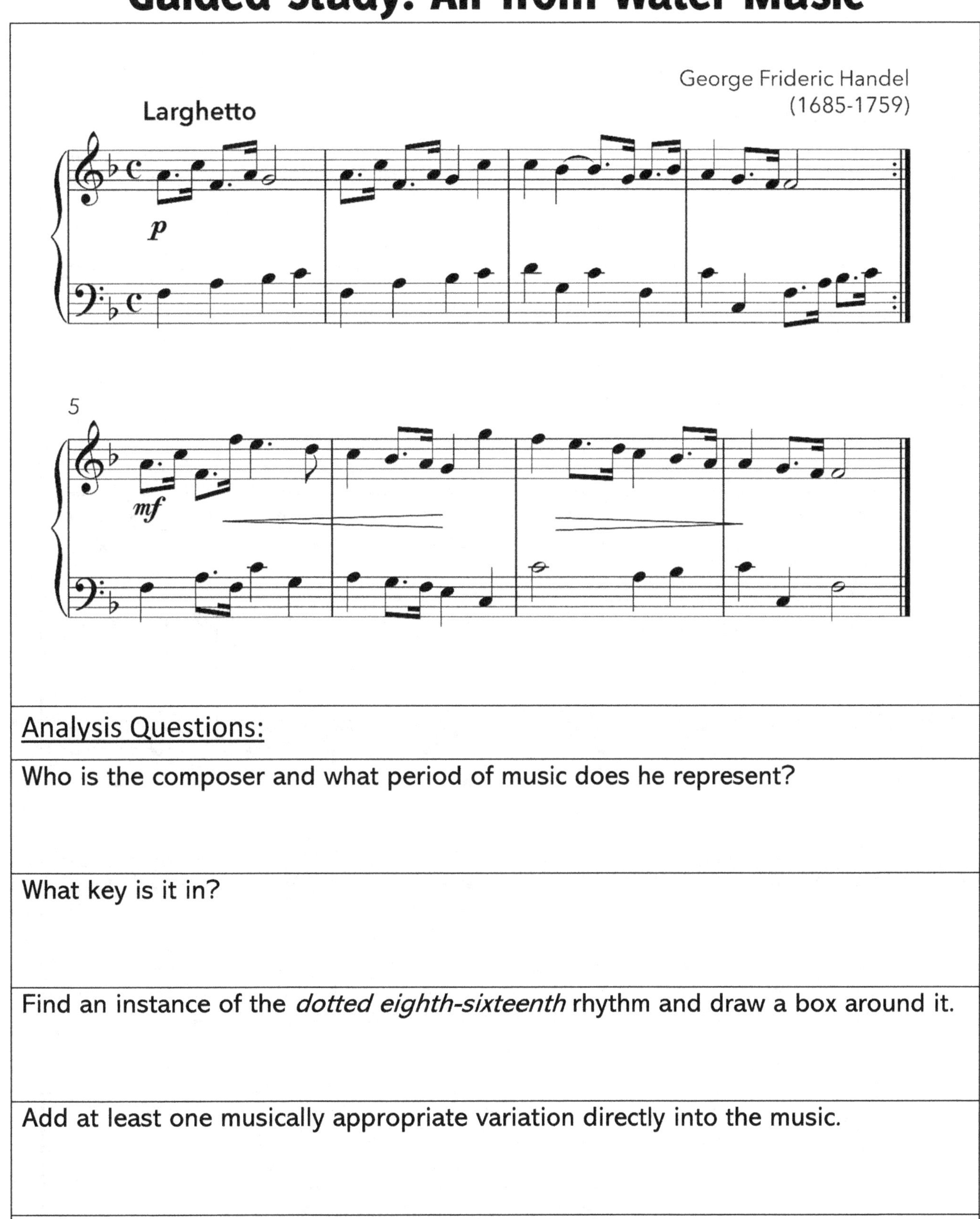

Analysis Questions:

Who is the composer and what period of music does he represent?

What key is it in?

Find an instance of the *dotted eighth-sixteenth* rhythm and draw a box around it.

Add at least one musically appropriate variation directly into the music.

What does the tempo say and what does it mean?

Guided Study: The Bear

Analysis Questions:
Who is the composer and what period of music does he represent?
In what measure does the **tenuto** articulation first appear?
What underlying scale is the song built on?
Directly into the music, add at least one musically appropriate variation.
What aspects of the music help represent a "bear," in your opinion?
(doodle space)

Harmony: Chords

Melody vs Harmony:
Named Chords:
Chords by Name:
Which element of music is recognizable as the "song?"
A melody is built using scales. What is harmony built using?
What are the four essential chord types?

Three Note Chords

Intervals Review:
Major Chords:
Minor Chords:
Diminished Chords:
Augmented Chords:
Describe the quality of a major chord.
Describe the quality of a minor chord.
Describe the quality of a diminished chord.
Describe the quality of an augmented chord.

Four Note Chords

7th Chords:

Added Notes:

Simplifying a Chord:

What is the most commonly used 7th chord?

What are two "safe" notes to add as a variation to a major chord?

What are the notes of a G7 chord?

Lead Sheets

Beautiful Dreamer

Stephen Foster

Down By the Riverside

Traditional

Chord Charts and Symbols:
Lead Sheets:
Chord Progressions:
Go through the given lead sheets. Attempt to play all the chords listed in block form. Try both hands.
Try to play the melodies of each lead sheet. Pay special attention to trying to decode the rhythms and how they fit with the meter.

Study: Block Form Lead Sheet

Go Tell It On the Mountain

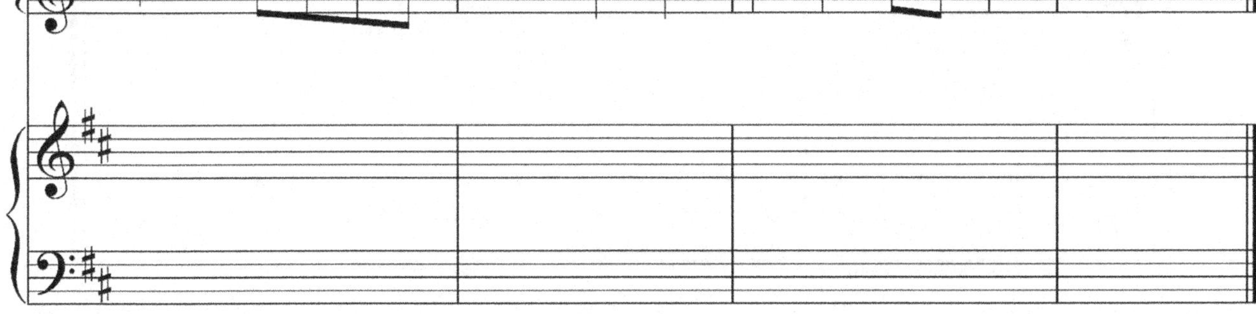

Write block chords into the lead sheet above using the provided chord chart.

Practice playing the chords and the melody separately, then together.

Try playing a block chord arrangement of another lead sheet without writing anything down.

Guided Study: The Love and Pleasure of a Thing Make All the Work and Labor Nothing

from *60 Progressive Pieces for Piano,*
Op. 60, No. 10

Daniel Gottlob Turk
(1756-1813)

Allegretto

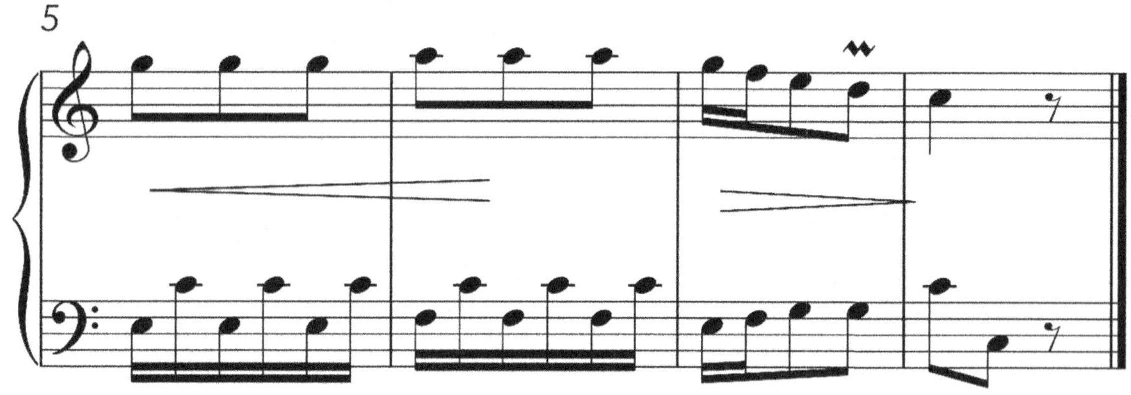

Analysis Questions:
How many **beats per measure**?
Translate the **tempo**.
What **key** is it in?
What **chord** do the notes in the 1st **measure** form?
What is the **ornament** in **measure 7** and what does it mean?

Guided Study: The Gamut

from *60 Progressive Pieces for Piano,*
Op. 60, No. 6

Daniel Gottlob Turk
(1756-1813)

Allegro non troppo

mp

5

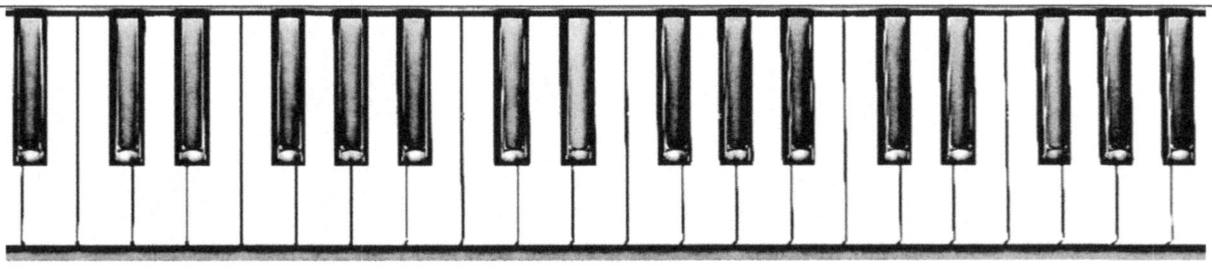

Analysis Questions:
What **key** is it in?
What is the **tempo**?
What is the **highest note**?
What is the **lowest note**?
Write the **measure number** above each measure.

Daniel Gottlob Türk (1750-1813) was a German composer, music theorist, and influential piano teacher of the Classical era. His progressive pieces for piano hold great importance as they pioneered piano pedagogy, focusing on a gradual progression of difficulty to help students develop their technical skills and musical expression. These pieces were accessible to pianists of different levels and influenced other composers like Beethoven, Czerny, and Clementi, shaping the way piano music was composed and taught in the 18th and 19th centuries. Additionally, Türk's compositions provide valuable insights into the performance practices and stylistic characteristics of the Classical era, offering a glimpse into the musical world of that time. They remain essential resources for piano students and performers, aiding in the honing of their skills and understanding of the musical heritage.

Guided Study: Turk's Lullaby

from *60 Progressive Pieces for Piano,*
Op. 60, No. 18

Daniel Gottlob Turk
(1756-1813)

Analysis Questions:
What is the **key?**
Write in the **notes** in both hands **in measure 3**.
What are the **lowest** and **highest notes**? Include the **register** or octave number.
Add your own **articulations** to the sheet music in a way that you think captures the character of the piece.
Diagram the **beats** in measure 5.

The Circle of Fifths

Circle of Fifths Review:

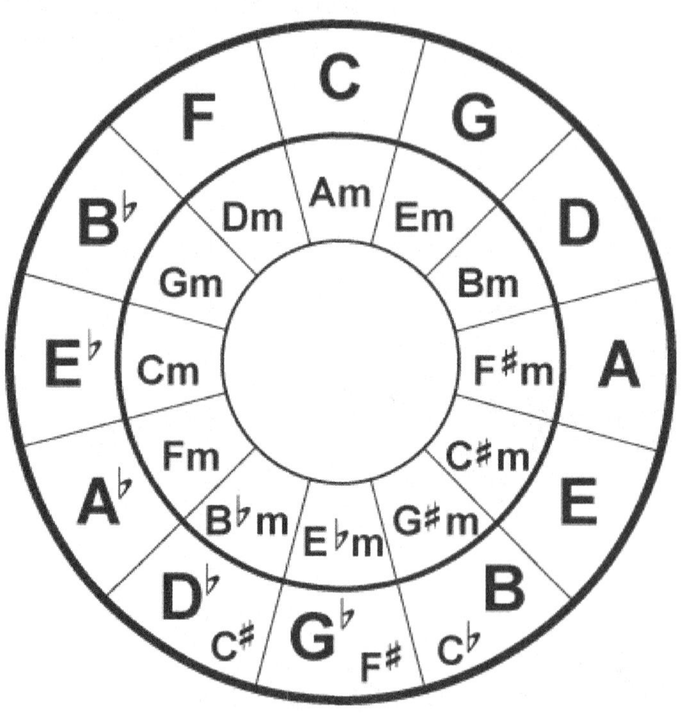

Relationships Between Keys:

Keys and Levels:

Minor Scales

Review:

The Minor Scale:

Intervals of a Minor Scale:

Questions:
How many different types of minor scales are frequently used?
Which is the type that we worked on today?
Which natural minor scale as no black keys?
Identify the correct keys for a *C minor scale.*
(doodle space)

Melodic and Harmonic Minor

The Melodic Minor Scale:

The Harmonic Minor Scale:

Questions:

Which type of minor is most commonly used in today's world?

Which minor scale has different intervals going up and down?

Why do singers not tend to like the harmonic minor scale?

Identify the correct keys the *A harmonic* minor scale.

(doodle space)

The Keys of G Major and F Major

G Major:

F Major:

Guided Study: Aura Lee

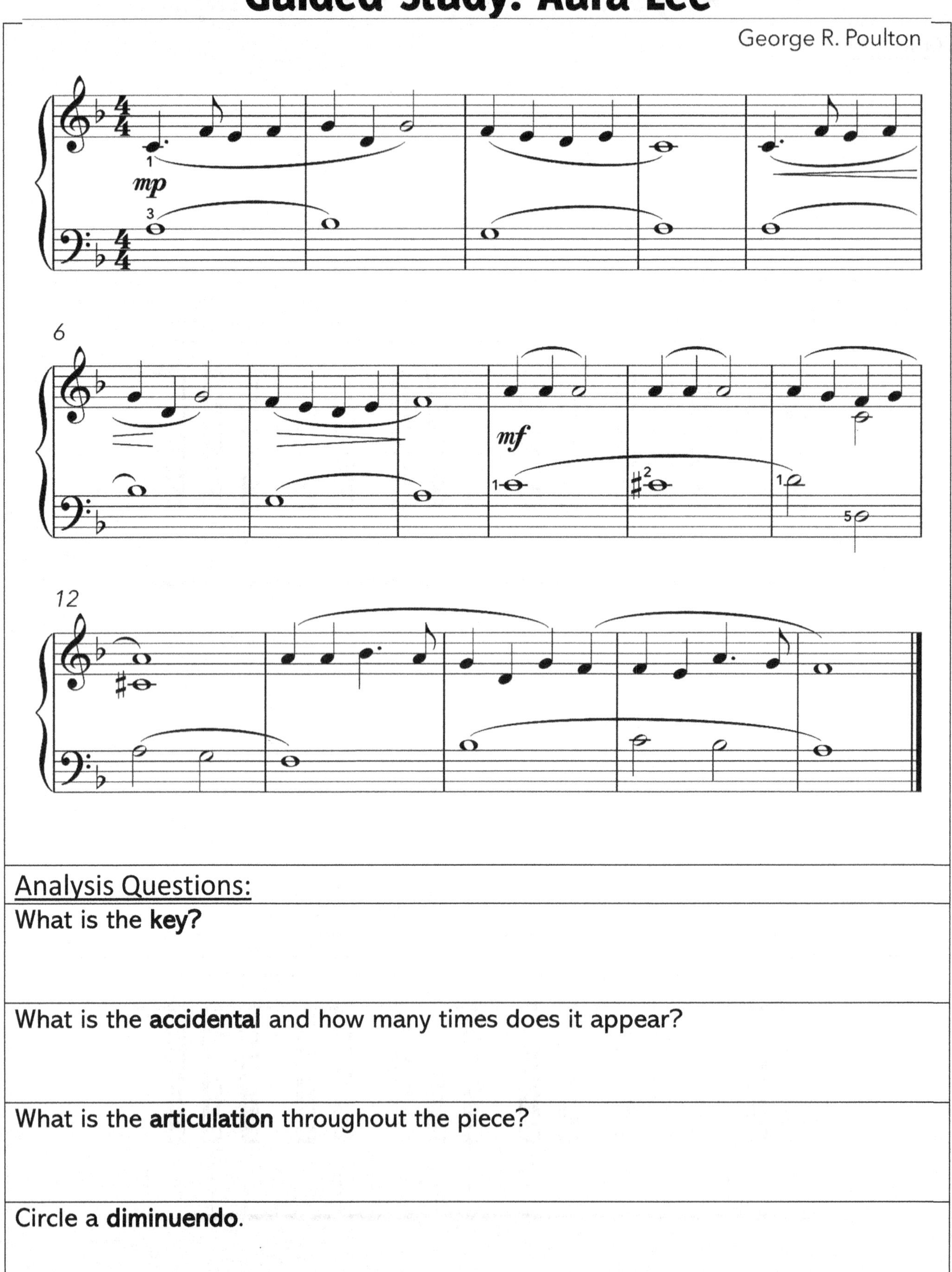

Analysis Questions:

What is the **key?**

What is the **accidental** and how many times does it appear?

What is the **articulation** throughout the piece?

Circle a **diminuendo**.

The Keys of E minor and D minor

E minor:

D minor:

The Keys of D Major and B♭ Major

D Major:

B♭ Major:

The Keys of B minor and G minor

B minor:

G minor:

History Review: Baroque Period

Baroque Characteristics:
Baroque Composers:
Listening Reflections:

Minuet in D minor

from *Notebook for Anna Maagdalena Bach*,
BWV Anh. 132

History Review: Classical Period

Classical Characteristics:
Classical Composers:
Listening Reflections:

Minuet in F

K. 2, from *Nannerl's Music Book*

Wolfgang Amadeus Mozart
(1756-1791)

History Review: Romantic Period

Romantic Characteristics:
Romantic Composers:
Listening Reflections:

'Modern' Timeline

20th Century Art Music

Art Music vs Folk Music:
Modernism and Modern Schools:
Post Questions:
What made **modernism** different from **Romanticism**?
Which of the schools explored local folklore or folk music and the history, myths and legends of their own nation?
Give an example of **experimental music**?

Tempo Gusto from Hungarian Rhapsody No. 2

F. Liszt

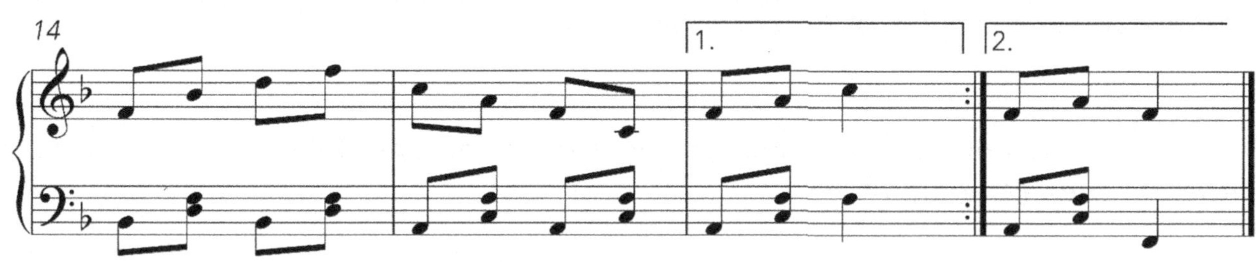

20th Century Popular Music

American "Melting Pot":
Music Industry:
Post Questions:
What are a few examples of **American folk music**?
What musical techniques had origins in the African and Caribbean traditions instead of the European tradition?
What is a "blue" note?

The Entertainer
Scott Joplin
(1868-1917)
♩ = 62
mp
p
f
p
f
mp

Soundtrack Music

Soundtrack Music:
Soundtrack Composers:
Post Questions:
When was the first appearance of a soundtrack in movies?
How do movies help keep older traditions of music alive?
How does music enhance the storytelling in film?

The Rat Pack

The Rat Pack:
1900
1910
1920
1930
1940
1950
1960
1970
1980
1990
2000

Peter Lawford:
Sammy Davis, Jr:
Frank Sinatra:
Dean Martin:
Joe Bishop:

The British Invasion

The British Invasion:

The Beatles:
Herman's Hermits:
The Rolling Stones:
Donovan:
Tom Jones:
Dusty Springfield:

Disco and Hip Hop

Disco:

1900 1910 1920 1930 1940 1950 1960 1970 1980 1990 2000 2010

Saturday Night Fever:

Donna Summer:

Hip Hop:
Old-School Hip Hop:
New-School Hip Hop:
Golden Age Hip Hop:

Teen Pop

Teen Pop:
1900
1910
1920
1930
1940
1950
1960
1970
1980
1990
2000

Jackson Five:
New Kids on the Block:
Backstreet Boys:
Christina Aguilera:
Taylor Swift:

Section III: Readings

Internalization

What Does It Mean to Have Something Internalized?

To have something internalized means it has become a natural or automatic part of you. It no longer requires thought or effort; it happens automatically when needed or desired. When achieved, you might say what you have internalized has become a part of your **active self** or personality.

Usually, it takes a very long time to internalize something. To achieve internalization requires effort, interest, and repetition, but once it is internalized these are no longer required. When something is internalized it is easy and natural, and seems more like a talent than something that has been learned. Both mental and physical things can be internalized, though the process is not exactly the same.

How Much Should I Practice?

The goal of practice is always to internalize something physical. Practice requires moving around, as it is impossible to internalize something physical without moving, but that does not mean it is the same as exercising. Also, practice does not really mean repeating things over and over and over again exactly the same (although repeating it is usually required). Instead practice means that you are trying to make physical motions more and more automatic, so that you don't have to think about them at all.

So, it is less about how *much* you should practice, and more about whether it is becoming or has become automatic.

Do I Need to Study?

The goal of study is also always to internalize, but instead of physical things, we study to internalize mental things. Studying requires thinking, as it is impossible to internalize something mental without thinking about it, but that does not mean it is the same as memorizing. Studying does not require moving around, though moving around might be helpful to study some things. But study is certainly not exercising muscles.

We want mental things often to be as automatic as physical things. Yes, studying is required, until certain concepts, thoughts, or inner models are internalized and appear in the mind automatically.

Goal-Oriented Study and Practice:

Remember, the goal is always to internalize. Learning is only temporary until you have reviewed material enough that you are able to access it automatically. Whether you are studying a concept, memorizing information, or improving a physical routine, mastery only comes when it has become a part of your active self.

Once something has been mastered, you can think more critically, consider more deeply, see solutions more intuitively, and operate with ease. Internalization allows you to rely on the foundation you have learned, so that you can achieve the real goal in performance: truly engaging with the material as though you have become one with it.

Post Questions:
What is the difference between study and practice?
How do you know if something has been internalized?
Is it more necessary to practice (and internalize physical things) or to study (and internalize mental things)? Justify your answer.
What is the single goal of both study and practice?

N	O	I	T	A	Z	I	L	A	N	R	E	T	N	I	Y	T
U	L	A	C	I	S	Y	H	P	W	N	E	M	F	T	P	I
J	V	M	A	Z	P	W	R	D	F	A	C	O	L	U	E	N
L	Q	K	D	O	P	G	R	O	V	K	I	D	E	X	R	F
A	R	E	P	E	T	I	T	I	O	N	T	E	S	L	F	O
T	B	Z	C	M	C	F	I	R	E	E	C	L	E	C	O	R
N	X	Y	I	P	I	N	O	Y	C	Y	A	P	V	O	R	M
E	J	U	L	M	T	R	A	U	R	N	R	K	I	N	M	A
M	O	U	X	E	A	L	Z	T	N	E	P	P	T	C	A	T
S	O	Y	D	Y	M	M	B	H	U	D	T	P	C	E	N	I
X	D	T	D	U	O	O	D	H	T	R	A	S	A	P	C	O
C	I	U	R	N	T	V	U	M	A	F	A	T	A	T	E	N
Y	T	E	V	N	U	I	D	E	I	R	A	L	I	M	U	L
S	T	N	E	G	A	N	R	U	I	K	T	P	U	O	E	I
M	T	Q	E	O	T	G	T	H	I	N	K	I	N	G	N	B

mastery repetition moving physical active self automatic
internalization performance foundation information mental
thinking natural practice study model concept

The Active Practice Method

The **active practice method** is a specific method that provides a flexible, efficient, and reliable way to improve by focusing on specific parts of what you're learning and repeating them in very particular ways. This method is designed to help you thoroughly learn and **internalize** performances, whether they are music pieces, drama monologues, or any other type of presentation. A key part of this method is concentrating on specific aspects of the self or the repertoire, known as **active targets**, and repeatedly practicing sections of your performance with a strong understanding of the conscious, the subconscious, and how they fit together. This focused and strategic repetition helps you gain a deeper and more detailed understanding of the pieces you are performing, and enhances your ability to execute them from a subconscious place of mastery rather than through conscious control.

Remember, the best performance comes from the action of the subconscious, not the conscious, as advanced performance repertoire is too complex for the conscious mind to control while still achieving relaxed flow. Instead, the active practice method understands that almost all aspects of the performance will happen unconsciously in a final performance, and therefore focuses on the relationship between the conscious and subconscious as a student works toward a final performance.

The Method

At its core, the active practice method involves a systematic process of repetition (a multi-iterative cycle) with a focused intent. Performers begin by selecting a piece of their repertoire, which could range from a segment of a musical score to a portion of a script. The key to this method lies in the selection of an **active focus** or **target**. This target is a single aspect of the performance that can be attended to by the performer — from emotional expression and technical precision to character motivation or musical dynamics.

Once a performer picks an active focus, they practice the chosen part of their piece *between four and seven times*, concentrating fully on that specific focus. After finishing these repetitions, they pick a new focus and repeat the process. This cycle keeps going, with the performer switching focuses until their practice session is over. Learning about different kinds of focuses and how they help in deeply learning the material is a key part of getting better at practicing.

It's crucial to understand that the details of the active practice method are designed to achieve various psychological effects. The method can be tweaked to suit each individual over time, but getting to know, appreciate, and recognize these effects will help in mastering the method more fully. The aim is for students to learn how to gain more control and understanding of how to deliberately absorb results through the process of **sublimation** (the transfer of things from the conscious mind to the subconscious mind).

Psychological Effects

The effectiveness of the method is rooted in several psychological phenomena:

1. Engaging the **trance effect**: By repeating a piece exactly the same way several times, performers can enter a state called the trance effect. This state involves two main features: the process becomes automatic, and the conscious mind finds it harder to focus on the target. As the trance effect takes hold, the sequence they are practicing starts to feel more natural and effortless, becoming more deeply embedded in the performer's skills. The shorter the section of the performance repeated, the more likely the trance effect will occur.
2. Resetting the **boredom effect**: By constantly choosing new mental targets, this method helps avoid the boredom that usually comes with doing the same thing over and over. Even though you're physically repeating the same actions, changing what you focus on mentally keeps your mind active and sharp. This makes the practice time more effective and improves the quality of your learning.
3. **Sublimation** of changing targets: As you switch from one target to another, the effects of each target subtly build up. Each target adds a small layer or echo that gets absorbed into your skills and the piece you are practicing, making both richer and more complex over time. This layering process results in a performance that has detailed interpretations and expressions, and it helps you as a performer to keep growing in skill and insight. However, the true sublimation of a target doesn't start until your focus shifts to a new one, so it's important to keep changing targets to make this happen.
4. Efficient and adaptable **internalization**: This method makes learning and remembering your performance pieces more efficient because it cuts down on unnecessary repetition. It also keeps the process adaptable; by constantly changing what you focus on, you get to explore different parts of what you're performing. This approach helps you become more versatile and dynamic in your performances.

The active practice method allows the performer to master the art of practice itself, not just the repertoire being performed. By harnessing the power of focused repetition and the strategic selection of active targets, performers can achieve a more profound and nuanced mastery of their repertoire. This method not only streamlines the process of internalizing performance pieces but also enriches them with depth and adaptability. For actors, musicians, and performers across various disciplines, this method offers a pathway to achieving excellence, marked by precision, emotional depth, and technical proficiency. As they embrace this approach, performers can expect to see significant growth in their artistic capabilities, culminating in performances that resonate with authenticity and skill.

Post Questions:
Describe an activity in which you have experienced the **trance effect**. How did it affect the activity?
How does continually changing the **active focus targets** help in overcoming the challenges of repetitive practice?
Provide an example of an **active focus target** that might be helpful for you right now in your own work?
Which psychological effect of active practice do you think could make the biggest difference in your own work? Why?
Describe what is meant by the word **sublimation** in your own words.
How many times should an active practice be repeated?
Why does a masterful performance rely on the subconscious instead of the conscious mind?
How does choosing a new target help make a previous target subconscious?

Cultures and Traditions of Music

Music is a product of **culture**, and because culture changes over time, so does music. Culture includes all of the social norms of a society, including knowledge, beliefs, customs, and art forms. Music, like other art forms, takes ideas from the current culture and arranges them for entertainment, ritual, or some other purpose.

Different cultures have different tastes. An art form will represent those tastes. Since different cultures also have different values, what is considered "good" or "great" may be different for different cultures.

Culture is passed from generation to generation through various **traditions**. A tradition is a set of ideas, values, or rituals that is shared through several generations. Most traditions evolve over time and can change in details but share essential common values or routines. The music we learn about, broadly speaking, is part of a tradition of European Classical Music that goes back to the Middle Ages. This tradition includes a common selection of notes, a shared lineage of instruments, and a growing repertoire of music and musical vocabulary built from these that we enjoy. It has continued uninterrupted since the creation of the music staff led to a common way of writing music down.

Other traditions, such as Chinese traditional music, Indian classical music, Cambodian ceremonial music, etc, still exist today all over the world. These traditions come from different cultures with different expectations, different notes (in many cases), different instruments, different performance rituals, and different ways of notating music. It would be difficult for us to fully appreciate these traditions of music without first adjusting our expectations and listening until we get used to the different sounds of their instruments and the different types of scales, chords, and other musical devices they employ.

The rise of certain technologies, including audio recording and the internet, has helped to merge traditions over the last hundred years. Since around 1900, we have been able to record and distribute music all over the globe, and since 2000 it has become easy for anyone to listen to music from any recorded tradition in history online through websites and apps such as YouTube, Spotify, or Pandora.

This has led to a proliferation of styles and **genres**. These mini-traditions focus on certain aspects of the larger tradition and allow individuals to easily find music that fits their taste. Different genres such as rock, R&B, gospel, techno, and such all use the same essential notes, basic rhythmic ideas, and sonic vocabulary going all the way back to the Middle Ages. In today's world, these genre labels can help identify commonalities in different pieces from our ongoing European classical tradition, which because of internet technology has expanded to much of the globe. Most music globally is now written with classical European symbols and evaluated to some degree to classical European standards, though many cultures and musicians work hard to protect their own traditions and keep them alive for future generations.

Post Questions:
What is the current dominant **tradition** of music called?
When did it begin?
What is the difference between a **tradition** and a **genre**?
What are a couple examples of **music traditions**?
What are a couple examples of **music genres**?
Why have the last 100 years led to a lot of changes in our tradition?
How is a culture different from a tradition?
What are some values and beliefs that are a part of our current **culture**?
What are some ways we could gain an appreciation of a music tradition that is different from our own?
What factors have helped our music tradition continue uninterrupted for a thousand years?

The Baroque Period

The **Baroque period**, spanning from approximately 1600 to 1750, marks an era of grandeur and complexity in the world of music. This era, known for its ornate style and elaborate ornamentation, laid the groundwork for the expressive capabilities of the piano, even though the instrument was in its nascent stages of development.

Baroque music is characterized by its dramatic energy, contrasting textures, and the greater use of ornamentation. Unlike the relatively straightforward melodies of the Renaissance, Baroque music embraced complexity and emotional depth. Composers of this period sought to evoke intense feelings through their music, often using a technique known as the 'doctrine of affections', where each piece or movement was intended to arouse a specific emotion in the listener.

The Harpsichord and the Clavichord

The **harpsichord**, known for its bright and penetrating sound, was a centerpiece in many Baroque compositions. Unlike the **piano**, which produces sound by hammers striking strings and wasn't invented until late in the Baroque period, the harpsichord generates its unique timbre through quills plucking strings when its keys are pressed. This mechanism, while limiting the instrument's ability to vary the loudness of notes, contributed to its signature crisp and resonant tone, making it ideal for performing in large, resonant spaces such as churches and palatial halls.

The harpsichord's ability to sustain notes also influenced Baroque compositions, leading to a focus on intricate melodies and complex harmonic structures. Its sound was particularly suited to the polyphonic texture of Baroque music, where multiple, independent melodic lines interweave to create a rich tapestry of sound. The instrument's prominence is reflected in the works of composers like Handel and Bach, who composed numerous harpsichord suites and concertos, utilizing the full range and capabilities of the instrument.

In contrast to the grandeur of the harpsichord, the **clavichord** offered a more subtle and expressive experience. Its mechanism, involving metal tangents striking the strings to produce sound, allowed for greater dynamic control, enabling the player to express nuances in volume and articulation by varying the touch. This made the clavichord a preferred instrument for private practice and intimate performances, where its delicate and nuanced sound could be fully appreciated.

The clavichord's ability to produce a sustained tone, albeit softer than the harpsichord, was cherished by composers and players for its expressive capabilities. It was particularly favored for its ability to execute vibrato-like effects, known as 'bebung,' which added emotional depth to the music. Composers like Carl Philipp Emanuel Bach, a son of J.S. Bach, were known for their affinity towards the clavichord, using its expressive potential to its fullest in their compositions.

The harpsichord and clavichord played a critical role in shaping the development of the piano. The piano, invented in the early 18th century by Bartolomeo Cristofori, sought to combine the dynamic versatility of the clavichord with the sound projection of the harpsichord. The evolution of these instruments and their distinctive qualities significantly influenced the compositional styles of the Baroque period and beyond, paving the way for the piano to become the versatile and expressive instrument we know today.

Influential Composers

Several key composers defined the Baroque era, each contributing uniquely to the evolution of music.

Johann Sebastian Bach, a towering figure of this period, was known for his profound understanding of music theory and ability to weave intricate musical tapestries. His works, such as the "Well-Tempered Clavier," are celebrated for their intellectual depth and technical brilliance. His children continued to influence music in the Classical period after his death.

George Frideric Handel, another luminary of this era, gained immense popularity for his operatic works and oratorios. His music, known for its expressive melodies and grandiose style, was widely appreciated by audiences across Europe.

Domenico Scarlatti, an Italian composer, brought a distinctively fresh perspective with his keyboard sonatas. His compositions, brimming with Iberian influences and innovative techniques, significantly influenced the development of keyboard music.

Antonio Vivaldi, primarily known for his violin concertos, also contributed to keyboard music. His fast-paced, rhythmically vibrant style added a new dimension to the music of this period.

Post Questions:

How long ago did the **Baroque period** begin?

What are typical characteristics of the **Baroque** style?

Which composer's children continued to influence music in the Classical period?

Describe the difference in sound between the **harpsichord** and the **clavichord**?

Why wasn't the piano a common instrument in the Baroque period?

The Classical Period

The **Classical period** in piano music, spanning roughly from 1750 to the early 1820s, marks a significant evolution in the world of music, characterized by a shift towards clarity, order, and balance. This era, often seen as a reaction against the complex and ornamented Baroque style, brought about fundamental changes in musical composition and performance, paving the way for the modern piano and its repertoire.

One of the most striking aspects of the Classical Period was the transformation in the design and capabilities of keyboard instruments. The **fortepiano**, an early version of the modern piano, emerged during this time. Invented by Bartolomeo Cristofori in the early 18th century, it rapidly gained popularity due to its ability to produce a wider range of dynamics compared to its predecessors, the harpsichord and clavichord. The fortepiano's unique action mechanism allowed for greater expressive control, enabling pianists to play both soft **(piano)** and loud **(forte)** passages, a feature not possible with earlier keyboard instruments.

The music of the Classical Period was marked by a more homophonic texture, a contrast to the polyphony of the Baroque era. Melody became the focus, supported by a clear harmonic structure. This period also saw the development of well-defined musical forms, such as the sonata, symphony, and concerto, which provided a framework for composers to explore musical ideas with greater depth and coherence.

Influential Composers

Several key composers were central to defining the Classical style.

Wolfgang Amadeus Mozart, a child prodigy who became one of the most prolific and influential composers of the era, is known for his elegant and expressive compositions that include piano concertos, sonatas, and chamber works. His music, characterized by its melodic beauty and formal perfection, remains a staple in piano education and concert repertoire.

Ludwig van Beethoven, often credited with bridging the Classical and Romantic periods, expanded the expressive range of the piano through his innovative compositions. His piano sonatas, like the famous 'Moonlight Sonata,' showcase a dramatic use of contrast, dynamic range, and structural complexity. Beethoven's music not only pushed the boundaries of the instrument but also of the musical form, laying the groundwork for the emotive style of the Romantic era.

Joseph Haydn, another prominent figure of this period, contributed significantly to the development of piano music. Known as the 'Father of the Symphony' and 'Father of the String Quartet,' Haydn also wrote numerous piano sonatas and chamber works that are celebrated for their form, clarity, and wit.

The Classical Period also witnessed the rise of public concerts, shifting music from the private chambers of the aristocracy to concert halls and public spaces. This change broadened the audience for piano music and increased the demand for pianists and composers.

For piano students, the Classical period offers a rich and essential foundation that shapes their understanding and appreciation of the piano. This era, with its emphasis on clarity, balance, and structure, provides an ideal starting point for developing the skills and sensibilities necessary for proficient piano playing.

One of the hallmarks of Classical music is its use of **phrasing** – the way notes are grouped together to create a musical sentence. Learning to play Classical pieces helps students understand how to shape a phrase, how to build tension and release it, and how to use dynamics to highlight the emotional content of the music. This skill is crucial as it goes beyond the technical aspect of playing notes and delves into the expressive, interpretative side of piano playing.

Classical music, with its well-defined structures such as sonatas, concertos, and symphonies, offers students a clear framework within which to develop their technical skills. The melodies in Classical pieces are often straightforward yet elegant, requiring students to focus on precision and clarity of expression. This precision is not just about playing the right notes; it's about understanding the phrasing, dynamics, and articulation that bring a piece to life. For instance, a Mozart sonata, with its articulate melodic lines and nuanced **dynamics**, challenges students to develop control and subtlety in their playing.

Post Questions:

How long ago did the **Classical period** begin?

How did the Classical period respond to the Baroque style? What are common Classical qualities?

Which of the Classical composers is credited for bridging the Classical and Romantic periods?

What aspects of Classical music make it ideal for early piano study?

Why was the piano preferred in the Classical period over previous keyboard instruments?

The Romantic Period

The **Romantic period** in piano music, spanning from the late 18th century to the early 20th century, represents a profound shift in the musical landscape, reflecting broader changes in art, literature, politics, and society. This era, fueled by the spirit of individual expression and emotional depth, brought about a significant transformation in piano composition and performance, offering a rich tapestry of exploration for beginning piano students.

As a reaction against the restraint and formality of the Classical era, Romantic music is characterized by its expressive intensity and individualism. Composers sought to convey deep emotions and personal experiences through their music, often inspired by nature, literature, and their own internal struggles. This period saw the **piano** become a powerful vehicle for emotional expression, largely due to its dynamic range and expressive capabilities, which were continually enhanced through technological advancements in piano construction.

The Romantic era coincided with significant societal changes. The **Industrial Revolution** brought about new ideologies and a shift in social structures. In art and literature, there was a move towards expressing more personal, introspective, and often turbulent emotions, mirroring the political upheavals and cultural shifts of the time. These themes found their way into piano music, as composers used the instrument to express a broader range of human emotions than ever before.

Composers and Concerts

Several key composers dominated this period, each bringing their unique voice and perspective to piano music. There are perhaps more well-known composers from this period than any other, as interest in individualized expression led music in a variety of direction. In particular, the piano saw a tremendous amount of development in the repertoire of this period.

Frédéric Chopin, known for his poetic genius and technical refinement, focused almost exclusively on the piano, producing a wealth of waltzes, nocturnes, ballades, and etudes. His music, with its intricate melodies and expressive nuances, captures the essence of Romanticism's introspective and expressive depth.

Franz Liszt, a virtuoso pianist and composer, expanded the technical and expressive possibilities of the piano. His compositions, marked by their dramatic flair and technical brilliance, pushed the boundaries of the instrument, inspiring a generation of pianists and composers. Liszt's contribution to the symphonic poem and his thematic transformation techniques reflected the Romantic era's integration of music with other art forms, particularly literature.

Johannes Brahms, another towering figure, brought a more structured approach to the Romantic ethos. His music, while emotionally rich, often harkened back to Classical forms, showing his reverence for composers like Beethoven. Brahms' piano works, including his concertos and sonatas, are celebrated for their lyrical beauty and structural complexity.

The Romantic Period also witnessed a change in the venues for musical performance. Public concerts became more widespread, moving away from private salons and courts to concert halls. This shift allowed a broader audience to experience the power and beauty of piano music.

The Romantic Period offers an expansive world of emotional expression and technical development. The period's music allows students to explore a wide range of dynamics, from the subtlest pianissimo to the most commanding fortissimo, and everything in between. The emphasis on expressive playing, with the use of rubato (flexible tempo) and varied articulations, helps students develop a deeper musical sensitivity and emotional connection to the music.

The Romantic Period also serves as an excellent introduction to the concept of programmatic music – compositions inspired by external narratives or ideas, often literary or natural. Understanding how music can depict a story or a scene encourages students to think about music more imaginatively and interpretively.

In piano music, with its rich interplay of emotion, technique, and narrative, the period offers beginning piano students a comprehensive platform for both technical development and expressive exploration. Romantic music is not just a collection of notes and rhythms; it's a gateway to understanding the deeper, more nuanced aspects of human expression and the powerful role that music can play in articulating those emotions.

Post Questions:

What were some of the societal changes that impacted musical development in this period?

What particular qualities and characteristics were admired during the **Romantic period**?

Which of the Romantic composers mentioned is known for his structured approach and use of **classical** forms?

What are some reasons Romantic music is useful for the developing piano player?

What is meant by the idea of **programmatic music**?

The Modern Period

The **Modern period** in piano music, which began in the late 19th century and extended through the 20th century, marks a time of extraordinary change and experimentation in the musical realm. This era, influenced by the rapid transformations in society, technology, art, and politics, witnessed a profound evolution in the way music was composed, performed, and perceived. For beginning piano students, the Modern period opens a window to a world of innovative techniques, diverse styles, and a deeper understanding of the piano's expressive capabilities.

In the Modern Period, composers broke away from the traditional tonalities and structures that had dominated Western music for centuries. Influenced by the broader artistic movements of the time, such as **impressionism**, **expressionism**, and **surrealism** in art, and the sweeping changes brought about by two World Wars and the technological revolution, music became a medium for exploring new ideas and expressing the complexities of the modern experience. Piano music, in particular, became a canvas for this exploration, with composers pushing the instrument's boundaries to create new sounds and textures.

Explorations in Tonality

One of the most significant trends of this period was the departure from traditional **tonality**. Composers like **Arnold Schoenberg**, who developed the **twelve-tone technique**, sought to create music that was free from the constraints of **major and minor scales**. This approach to composition opened up new possibilities for musical expression, although it could be challenging for listeners accustomed to the tonal music of previous eras.

Another notable figure of this period was **Igor Stravinsky**, whose music was marked by its rhythmic complexity and use of **dissonance**. Stravinsky's works, including his compositions for piano, were often bold and unconventional, reflecting the turbulent times in which he lived.

Claude Debussy and **Maurice Ravel**, prominent figures of the impressionist movement in music, brought a different perspective to piano composition. Their works are characterized by their use of non-traditional scales, such as the **whole-tone scale**, and their focus on tone color and atmosphere. Debussy's piano works, such as "Clair de Lune" and "Images," evoke vivid imagery and emotion through their subtle and nuanced use of harmony and texture.

The Modern period also saw the rise of American composers who contributed to the diversity of piano music. **George Gershwin**, for example, blended elements of **jazz** with traditional classical forms, creating a uniquely American sound in compositions like "Rhapsody in Blue."

The later part of the Modern period in piano music, particularly the mid to late 20th century, witnessed further groundbreaking changes, significantly influenced by the burgeoning music industry and the advent of new technologies. This era saw the emergence of new genres, the fusion of diverse musical styles, and the increased accessibility of music to a broader audience, all of which had a profound impact on the world of piano music.

With the advent of **electronic music** and advancements in recording technology, the later Modern Period brought an unprecedented level of experimentation and innovation. The development of **synthesizers** and electronic keyboards expanded the sonic possibilities of the piano, allowing composers and performers to explore new textures and timbres. This period also saw the rise of minimalist composers like **Philip Glass** and **Steve Reich**, whose works often featured repetitive, hypnotic patterns that contrasted with the complexity of earlier modern music. Their compositions, sometimes incorporating electronic instruments alongside traditional pianos, offered a fresh perspective on rhythm and harmony.

The rise of the music industry played a crucial role in shaping piano music during this time. The mass production and distribution of recorded music transformed the way people accessed and consumed music. Pianists and composers were no longer confined to concert halls and elite circles; they could now reach a global audience through records, radio, and television. This democratization of music led to the blending of classical piano traditions with popular music genres, giving rise to crossover artists who could straddle the classical and popular music worlds.

Post Questions:

What were some artistic movements that influenced music in this period?

How did early modern composers break away from previous traditions?

Which of the composers blended jazz with traditional forms to create a new style of American music?

What were some of the innovations of the later modern period that impacted keyboard players significantly?

Why might early modern music be challenging to a beginning piano student?

Intervals

Measuring Intervals:

In **music theory**, an **interval** is a measure of the distance between the **pitch** of two notes. Western music relies heavily on very specific intervals or sets of intervals to achieve the variety of harmonic and melodic effects that we enjoy as listeners. Notes at certain intervals when played simultaneously have pleasant, harmonious, or **consonant** sounds to our ears. Other intervals have the opposite effect, one of **dissonance**, where it seems like notes clash or are "wrong" in some way.

The 12 notes we currently use are all separated by the same distance in musical terms, called a **half-step** or **semi-tone**. Each key on the musical keyboard is a half-step away from its nearest neighbor. Whether that key is a white key or black key makes no difference. If you play each key from bottom to top in order, skipping no keys, including black and white, you are moving in half-steps up the keyboard. This distance, considered the smallest distance between two notes, was set long ago in history, and might even be called the foundation of our tradition.

There are other pitches between the notes of the keyboard, and some other instruments may be able to play them, but in general these **micro-tones** (as they are called) are not considered notes and, unlike semi-tones, do not form a central part of western music theory. Outside of micro-tones, almost all other aspects of harmony and melody in music can be discussed, analyzed, and identified using the measurement of half-steps and their associated measure, **whole steps**.

A whole step is simply the distance of two half-steps, as two halves equal a whole. Most of our melodies in western music move in either half-steps or whole-steps, and the various patterns, or combinations, of half-steps, whole-steps and other intervals create the characteristic or emotional content of the music.

Scales and Chords:

How far apart notes are, then, defines the content of the underlying music. Musicians, having long been aware of this, have arranged various patterns to create various effects and given them a variety of names to help distinguish them.

When notes are played one at a time, separately and individually, we hear what we call **melodies**, and these are defined by a regular pattern of intervals underlying them. In today's theory, we call these patterns modes or **scales**. If two different pieces of music seem to have the same underlying emotion or character, it's probable that they are built on the same scales.

When notes are played together, at the same time, we hear what we call **harmonies**. These, too, are defined by the pattern of intervals underlying them. We call these stacks of notes played together **chords**, and if two different moments in music seem to share the same underlying quality, it's very possible they share the same type of chord.

Learning the underlying patterns of intervals that create these scales and chords therefore allows a musician to more easily play new music built on those same structures, and even create their own compositions or arrangements if they wish.

Post Questions:
What is the distance between two notes called?
What is the difference between a half-step and a whole-step?
What is the difference between melody and harmony?
Which of the two (melody or harmony) is built on scales?
Which of the two (melody or harmony) is built on chords?
Which sounds pleasant to our ears: consonance or dissonance?

```
o e q o y t n a n o s n o c i t x
l b s u e d e n o t o r c i m h t
a s j k u l o m n o z a d m j e a
v r y i x q y l r e d o m s a o i
r d a d a f n f e w c q u p d r r
e r u a p o x u h m t y e a a y e
t o a d i s s o n a n t f c o c r
n h o t s g l d e o s v h o n e k
i c o q d e n u m f e a n a s n u
y m m s s r e r l c r t t i i o x
e q u t e o a a h a v s a t s t i
i w e t p h h c c c i j s i p i a
p p t d s c i t s d t u e c e m m
n a r c m f e i z i q i t t b e g
p v i i u r s c a l e g p m t s b
```

whole-step micro-tone consonant character dissonant
distance half-step harmony interval emotion semitone
scale melody chord pitch theory mode pattern

Scales and Modes

Modes and Scales

Though there are twelve different notes used in western music, most melodies do not use all twelve. In fact, most melodies use a specific set of notes and leaves others out. When learning keyboard as a beginner, you see very little use of the black keys. This is because at an early level we learn simple melodies that use only a few keys, and make sure to stay with the white keys for the sake of simplicity.

Even complex melodies, thought, still won't use all twelve notes, because the specific set of notes chosen has a lot to do with the mood, emotion, or character of the resulting melody. A happy melody will use a different set of notes than a sad melody. But two happy melodies will likely share the same set of notes, because the collected notes sounds happy together even before a specific melody is created.

Historically, this collection of notes that had a specific emotion or character was called a **mode**. Over time the word **scale** has come to mean mostly the same thing, especially when talking about modern music. For instance, we refer to the collection of notes that is mostly used for happy music as the **major scale** today, but it can also be referred to as the major mode (and used to have a more elaborate name, the **Ionian mode**). The collection of notes that is mostly used for sad music is called the minor scale or minor mode (and used to be called the **Aeolian mode**).

Major and Minor Scales

Major and **minor scales** are built on seven of the twelve notes. They are called "seven-note" scales, but there are other, less common scales, that use different numbers of notes.

Because **major scales** create happy music and **minor scales** can create sad music, using both of them in music means that a range of music can be played, everything from happy to sad. Because they represent these emotions so well, these have become the most common two scales used in today's music. There are other scales, certainly, but probably more than 90% of the music you listen uses primarily major and minor scales.

Since the same major scales are used to create all of the happy music we listen to, and the same minor scales are used for all the sad music, it is probably important or at least useful to learn and practice the scales before learning and practicing the individual pieces themselves. After all, almost all the pieces are just taking advantage of the same patterns of notes.

As we will see when we start building major scales, there are only twelve major scales (one for each key), and they all follow the same pattern. Similarly, there are only twelve minor scales, and they follow a slightly different pattern. If you master the individual patterns and are able to find or play the scales themselves easily, you will find it easier to play any music built on that scale and will also be able to make up music of your own with very specific emotional content.

Post Questions:
What used to be called **modes** are now called what?
What emotion is associated with the **major scale**?
What emotion is associated with the **minor scale**?
Of the twelve notes, how many are used for a major or minor scale?
How many different major and minor scales are there?
Why is it important to learn the scales before learning individual pieces?
Most of modern music is built on which two scales?

s s c o l l e c t i o n n i i y r
c e e y i x f j a y o m a j o r e
a v t v o e o n n n d o i f n u t
l l e n e d e a s r i t m a i z c
e e u a a n t u q a e e m n a l a
s w m j p i s o l y l t o n n e r
s t m i e v l c r o n i t o i c a
e e t o n p n o d y t s i a a i h
n m t j r o e y e o t a i m p t c
i o b s d h r k m a p d c v y c v
p d i o t o f e l e m n g i s a z
p e r s k n o t e s b e u u t r e
a r j p a c w m m f e s n u o p u
h h h a j m u s i c m s y e q s a

ionian pattern melody twelve theory practice seven
emotion collection happiness character sadness aeolian
mode minor notes major music scale mood

Index of Sheet Music

Sections:

Made in the USA
Columbia, SC
07 July 2025